WHEN YOU WERE A TEENAGER?

CAN YOU IMAGINE IF YOU WOULD

HAVE GROWN UP IN VIENNA

DURING WORLD WAR TWO?

READ ON

To my long suffering father, whose heart I broke when I left him.

All descriptions of events and people are based solely on the author's personal experiences and remembrances, to the best of his abilities.

Illustrations by the author

A BOY'S WAR

VIENNA 1945

A boys life during the last
three years of
the Second World War

BY ALFRED PENZ

WHY, WHERE, WHO

WE ARE BORN

WE CAN NOT CHANGE

WE CAN ONLY MAKE

THE BEST OF IT

WELCOME TO MY WORLD

Seven decades have passed and child soldiers are still being used in wars fought in many countries around the world. Here, I describe the adventures and trials of a group of Viennese boys during the last three years of the Second World War.

Everything in this book is based on my personal experience as one of those boys. Historical and geographical notes serve to bring the time and places into context. Since none of my friends in Vienna are still alive, and my memory for names is limited, I have taken license to change all but some salient names.

Vienna, the city and its inhabitants, suffered less trauma than some of the major German cities. Destruction was only 20% as compared to 95% in Berlin, Hamburg or Dresden, and loss of life was much less than suffered by London during the Blitz.

This Viennese palette, therefore, allows me to paint a somewhat less hopeless picture of everyday life during those days. Including our experience in Hungary shows that young boys will be young boys whenever you loosen the leash a bit.

I also hope to shine a light on a regime that followed its leader to the point of insanity. My personal objections were not political—I was too young for that—but a realization that due to my background, mentality, and physical disability, I could fall victim to it. There was no wheel in which I could fit as a cog.

Read on, dear reader. May you find the details as interesting as the message.

Alfred Penz, 2022

Table of Contents

AIR-RAID EARLY WARNING SYSTEM
Heavy formations of enemy bombers moving direction Vienna,
presently passing German border

AIR-RAID EARLY WARNING SYSTEM
Heavy enemy formations over Wiener Neustadt,
another group heading north towards Vienna

AIR-RAID EARLY WARNING SYSTEM
Woou Woou Woou Woou Woou Woou Woou Woou

The sirens wail, a grating high-low, high-low. War has reached us. It was expected. It had to come after the Allied landing in Sicily.

"Have you got your survival stuff?
Grab your bag and head for the shelter."

THE SCYTHE IN THE SKY

1

THE STAIRS TO the cellar wind down.
Like entering a tomb.
One bare spooky lightbulb glows.

There are about twenty of us down here, just our immediate family and some of our renters. I sit on a board, atop a pile of coal, next to my aunt Ria. A kerosene lamp casts eerie shadows. Our cellar is not a proper air-raid shelter, just the coal and utility cellar of a hundred year old house.

We can hear everything going on outside. Only the wooden door of the coal chute separates us from above. It is quiet outside except for an air-raid warden yelling at someone.

Maybe they have gone somewhere else?

Then, there it is, the deep hum of many, many engines.

Tak…tak…tak, tak, tak…tak…tak

"Are they bombing?"

I think it is our flak. Two 15cm batteries are stationed on two massive flak towers, guided by a giant Wurzburg radar screen on top of a third tower. Flak towers, huge blocks of concrete, sheltering a city of scared humanity. Thousands huddled on benches, safe in the tunnel network of the towers. We are too far away to reach the towers in time.

Finally, the steady wail of the all-clear signal. This time it was easy. They bombed some factories at the periphery. They were too high up to be accurate. The target radius averages 3km, but you never know what they are going to hit.

This time our flak downed four of them over Vienna. Heavy, four-engine Liberator bombers bursting with death. This formation has probably already lost five on the way here and now they face the long way back to Africa, passing the gauntlet of German-held Italy. It is terrible for them too. In German, we call this a Himmelfahrtskommando (suicide mission), a ticket to heaven. But they will be back again and again. Life is no longer safe in Vienna or anywhere else in the Third Reich.

Every summer school holiday, my mother dispatches me to my grandmother in Aigen-Schlägl, a town at the top of Upper Austria's Mühlviertel. The venerable Westbahnhof, the Vienna Western Railway station, seems more active than ever. Many uniforms, the whole panoply of the Third Reich.

"Come, Fredi, we have to buy our tickets." We line up at the ticket wicket. "One adult and one child to Aigen-Schlägl, Oberdonau."

"That makes fifteen Mark, fifty six Pfennig and three Mark for the Winterhilfswerk. The train leaves from platform three in forty five minutes."

"Mama, look! Look at that crowd. They are all trying to get on our train."

Mother points to the door she wants. About ten people are outside it, trying to get on the train.

"Do not push, dear sir. Do not push."

"Jesus and the devil, take that Stradivarius out of my face!"

"Mister, you are cramming that suitcase right into the back of my knee!"

A military voice calls, "Quiet! Quiet, please. There is room for all of us, and there is a lot of time."

Mother is the queen of situations like this. With charm, a lovely smile, and plenty of panache, she gets us a prime spot right next to a window. The overhead bins are quickly filled up. Some altercations, rearranging. It cannot be helped that a few items end up on the floor between us, mainly the ones holding provisions.

I am wedged in between my mother and a heavy-set man with a party badge, brown suit, brown sweater, brown knickerbocker pants and brown shoes, shined to the point where they seem able to glow in the dark. He smells funny, kind of womanly, lavender or whatever they call the stuff. Turning sideways he accidentally pokes Mother.

My mother can become very regal.

"One does not poke a lady in Deutschland."

I am glad she did not say Austria. Hitler hates Austria.

The bloke in brown apologizes, "Forgive me, gracious lady."

My mother starts chatting with the Air Force master sergeant by the window opposite her. She is such a flirt sometimes, so embarrassing...

I decide that the best thing is to hold my tongue, listen, and people watch.

Next to the sergeant, the Stradivarius man clutches a violin case between his knees.

"I am the first violinist of the Bratislava symphony. I have a teaching assignment at the Salzburg Mozarteum. When I was a young man you could go by tramway from Bratislava to Vienna. Now it is such a pain."

A priest in a black cassock and one of those square, partitioned and tasseled Biretta caps sits by his side.

"Interesting," he says. "You now have a Catholic priest as leader of Slovakia. I met Dr. Tiso in Vienna."

Oblivious to Dr. Tiso, a corporal in the Luftwaffe uniform, anti-aircraft service, gazes at a very beautiful young girl in an Army uniform sitting opposite him.

Next to him, a small woman clutches a rucksack on her lap. Next to her, a blond girl, about my age. She winks at me. It would have been super to have her sitting next to me.

We hear the station master on the platform, "Train 368 to Salzburg, via St. Pölten, Amstetten, Linz. All aboard!"

A whistle. We are rolling.

On the other side of the man in brown, a railway-uniformed man on his way back to Russia speaks about the tremendous task of converting the Russian railway gauge to the German one.

Building the Atlantic Wall is taking millions of tons of cement and aggregates, all transported by rail. Added to to this are the ongoing disruptions caused by bombing and sabotage.

It is incredible what the Reichsbahn is able to achieve.

"Mama, what is a gauge?"

"I do not know, Fredi."

The sergeant opposite says, "The gauge is the distance between the wheels on the tracks. The Russians have a wider track."

A man in the far corner, black suit, short dark hair, and a narrow moustache like Hitler's, tries to unfold a large newspaper.

The Völkischer Beobachter. The party paper.

The woman opposite him holds a large paper-wrapped object. It must have taken several Völkischer Beobachter editions to artfully wrap the large parcel.

The compartment is full. Given the fact that at this stage of the war people are not as wide as they once were, we are still packed in like sardines. I count twelve in a compartment designed for ten. Many people are left in the corridors, some standing, some sitting on their luggage.

Somehow a conductor has made his way across the corridor obstacle course.

"Tickets, please!"

One by one, he punches tickets and examines marching orders. The man in the corner flashes a badge. The conductor stiffens. "Jawohl, Herr Kommisar!" The woman with the young girl doesn't hold her rucksack anymore, white-faced, she squeezes it.

As we get closer to St. Pölten, the woman with the paper-wrapped package says, "This is a beautiful, two hundred year old Meissen hundred-day clock. I am taking it to my aunt in St. Pölten."

She gets up and vanishes, her handbag slung across her shoulder and her package in her arms. We can hear her pleas in the corridor.

"This is a precious, historic object. I have to get off in St. Pölten. Please help me."

A very old man who appears to me to be over a hundred slides into her place. His appearance is very Austrian in a rustic sort of way.

"Grüss Gott."

The moustache across from him glowers but does not say anything. The only greeting allowed is 'Heil Hitler.'

The grinding sound of braking wheels. The train stops. We are in St. Pölten. Very few passengers get off or on.

Rolling again, the old man produces a beautifully carved, hooked pipe and seems to be looking for matches.

"Rauchen verboten!" hisses the policeman.

Farmers are notorious for insisting on smoking their putrid, uncured homemade tobacco. The old man calmly puts away his pipe, takes a round silver tin out of his pocket, opens it, and holds it out to the man opposite him.

"Care for some snuff?"

Mother is heavy in conversation with the sergeant who tells her about all the wonderful food he had in France. The talk about food makes me hungry. I have not eaten since breakfast. The party man in brown produces a knackwurst and nibbles on it. Everybody gazes at the knackwurst.

"Coupon 3 of the food ration card?" quips the man in the railway uniform.

"I work at the Braune Haus (Party Headquarters). I got some sausages directly from Gauleiter Bürckel."

It is awful to have to swallow a wonderful reply.

Outside the countryside looks peaceful, like war is just a dream. Amstetten is a small town, but it is an important railway junction. Approaching Amstetten, I see the first houses then—

WHAM!

A bomb goes off about ten metres away, alongside the train.

Wham, wham, wham

Wham, wham

More bombs.

"Get down as low as you can and cover your head with your arms!"

The train lifts on the track, shaking.

Will it derail?

Terror.

The compartment turns into a tangle of bodies screaming, pushing, and clawing for cover. Crying, some hysterics. A Hail Mary.

"Duck down, Fredi! Duck down!"

My mother covers me with her body. The sergeant seems to be on top of Mother.

A quiet voice says, "Relax, we are not dead yet."

Humans are amazingly resilient. Herd animals, we rally when threatened. Soon, people begin to help each other, calm each other. The train comes to an abrupt halt. The railway person and the policeman decide to investigate. In the adjacent compartment, a window is blown out. Some passengers are bleeding—just cuts from the broken glass.

An army captain fights his way along the corridors. "Stay in your places. The railway people know you are here."

Calm, heavenly calm. We have been lucky.

Mother clutches me and speaks quietly, "It is over, Fredi."

But it is not over

Wham, wham, wham
Wham, wham, wham, wham, wham, wham
Wham, wham, wham
Wham, wham, wham, wham, wham, wham
Wham, wham, wham
Wham, wham, wham, wham, wham, wham
Wham, wham, wham
Wham, wham, wham, wham, wham, wham

"They are carpet bombing the rail yard up ahead! Stay where you are!"

"Do not leave the train. Do not leave the train."

Rumours say the yard ahead resembles the craters of the moon. The railway official disappears for a while and comes back.

"The track will be repaired by tomorrow morning, so just relax."

He takes his place again. After a while, a soldier arrives with water and a medic to tend to the injuries.

We spend the night on a siding. Hard to sleep in such a crowd. Some loud snoring. The man with the party badge wheezes. I must have slept some. When I wake, the train is moving and the grey of early morning fills the compartment. Some houses burn in the distance.

And then as we proceed over the newly built railway embankment, a vista of horror—an endless panorama of huge craters is populated by hundreds of figures in blue-striped tunics. Figures in grey seemed to direct them. Surrealistically twisted railway tracks and scores of burned-out and dismembered rolling stock, surrounded by clusters of grey-skinned men with cutting torches. A locomotive exploded into parts, the pipes of its boiler gaping.

We see some of these blue-striped ghosts closer up. They move like zombies, exhausted, lifeless. But still, they are filling craters, straining under the heavy load of cut pieces of steel rail and debris.

A man in grey pokes the one nearest to him with the butt of his rifle. The zombies are inmates of the surrounding concentration camps. I feel sorry for them. I cannot help thinking about Herr Wotruba, the jovial barber who always had the latest jokes and candies for us kids. He listened to Radio London and the concierge heard him. He could be one of these people.

My God. I shudder, thinking that we could have been caught up in the middle of all this. A question of minutes. The train stops outside Amstetten to let off passengers. Arriving in Linz, most of us leave. The sergeant, the violinist, policeman, and priest remain. The flak soldier and the pretty girl sit next to each other holding hands. They are going to Salzburg together. We meet the rucksack lady and the girl my age standing in front of the station trying to hail a taxi.

"Where are you going?"

"Urfahr."

"So are we."

"Shall we share a taxi? It takes a bit for taxis to arrive and there are more and more people."

"Yes, with the alarms, the drivers take to the shelters."

We wait for about an hour and a half, sitting on a bench in front of the station. I finally get a chance to talk to the girl. Apart from my two female cousins, I rarely get time to socialize with girls.

"Are you going to school in Urfahr?"

"No, I go to a girls' school in Linz."

She is a year older than me. People in Linz take air-raids very seriously because of the huge Hermann Goring industrial complex close by.

Taxi!

We pile into the old Steyr 12. Linz looks the same.

The lady tells Mother, "I was scared to death that the man next to me was from the Gestapo. You know how they are about black market butchering. I have several kilos of lard and smoked meats with me which I got from my cousin in Stockerau. Every pig and chicken is accounted for. Even the farmers only get the standard rations. I might have just missed a one-way ticket to a concentration camp! I should not have told you that, but I am still so uptight."

At their small white house with a red door and a vegetable garden in front, Gerda and her mother get out.

"Nice to meet you, Fredi."

"Good luck, Gerda."

And after a short drive, there she is, the Mühlkreisbahn. A nineteen century relic, this narrow-gauge railway leads from Urfahr to Aigen-Schlägl. It will take two hours for the 50km trip. She will chuga-chuga-chuga, chaga-chaga-chaga, puffing up-hill and down-dale all the way to my hideaway from the war.

Take me to Grandma. To a bath, freshly baked doughnuts, regular meals, and the run of the countryside with its forests and large swimming hole. To joining my summer friends, Siegi and Pepi, and my cousins, Robert and Gerda.

No more war for the summer. What more could it take to create a boy's mini-paradise but to be away from this nasty war?

HUNGARIAN PASTORALE

2

DAD! MY SCHOOL has been chosen for a new Government Program called the KLV, the Kinderlandverschickung (Children's Evacuation). It is a program already in force at the major cities of the Reich to get children out of reach of the bombing. Look at this paper! My whole school class got it.

"Ethnic Germans in a small Hungarian town called Elék, close to the Romanian border, offered to take around a hundred thirteen year old boys, their teachers, and a Hitler Youth leader for a whole year. It is totally voluntary. Luck has it that Realgymnasium (my high school) was chosen. Dad, please, please let me go! Please!!"

"Well, I have to speak first with Mother, one or two of the teachers, and Aunt Ria. We will see. They will certainly feel that you will be safer there."

And thus began the first big adventure of my life.

It is happening. I am going to Hungary.

The train platform is crowded. The six volunteer teachers are:

Professor Ignaz Zelinski, our camp leader, will teach Chemistry and Physics

Professor Egon Wotruba, German and English

Professor Josef Trnka, History, Geography, and Technical Drawing

Professor Dr. Ilse Peter, Latin and French

Professor Hilde Wasserbauer, Biology, Art and Music

Our Hitler Youth leader, Siegfried Wessely, Physical Education and Sports

We are split into 6 groups, each one supervised by a teacher. Some parents are crying, others giving last-minute instructions. Everybody seems to be talking at the same time. The teachers are like tour guides, each waving a coloured flag above their head, shepherding their section of the flock.

Nobody has much baggage. We boys wear the Hitler Youth uniform which is still available on a separate ration card. On average, we have brought along two sets of outer clothing, three pairs of underwear, some handkerchiefs, boots, and a few selected school books. Even clothing is rationed. A pair of pants is five points on the Kleiderkarte (Clothing Card). There are ration cards for everything.

It is time to get aboard. There is no crowding. We stow our stuff in the overhead racks. The windows are pushed down, and everyone tries to lean out to reach parents' and friends' hands. A whistle. The train starts rolling. Much waving of dirty handkerchiefs.

We are off. We are off to live for a year in Hungary.

The Austrian countryside passes by, then a screeching of the train's brakes. We roll onto a sidetrack. On the main track, a seemingly endless train passes by—tanks, artillery, and passenger cars—an SS Division on the move.

The teachers produce a snack, a slice of Kommisbrot (stone-hard army bread) smeared with lard and an apple. Well, there might be butter in Hungary, we hope. The train slows down and stops. We are at the border. A border guard comes on the train, accompanied by a sombre-looking character in civilian clothes. The civilian makes Dr. Trnka open his suitcase.

Does he think Dr. Trnka is a spy?

He does not arrest Dr. Trnka or anyone else.

We roll into the Hegyeshalom station. We are in Hungary!

The Hungarian guards' uniforms are almost identical to Austria's old Kaiserlich-Königlich (Imperial and Royal) Army. Everyone is polite and friendly. In no time, we are on our way again, passing Györ toward Budapest.

The Budapest railway station is beautiful. It does not seem touched by war. Lots of uniformed people, the Honvéd—Hungary's military land force—of course, but also soldiers from the whole of the German Wehrmacht. Some Hungarian Arrow Cross members are clustered around a kiosk.

"Out, boys. Everyone out. We have to change trains."

"Check that you have not forgotten anything!" We are guided

across the busy station to the train with our reserved cars. "Here it is, our train to Békéscaba."

On the train, each teacher takes roll call of his or her assigned flock. After everyone is settled, more sandwiches appear. Pity, they are not Hungarian sandwiches, just the usual German army tackle with lard again and another apple.

Waiting in the corridor for the toilet, I get to talk to an SS man. He is on leave, going home to one of the German communities. He tells me that things are not going well on the Eastern Front.

"Yes," he says, "there has been some bombing in Hungary."

In Békéscaba, we change trains again. By now, we have become experienced travellers. Finally, the train stops at a small station. Elék—we have arrived! We have to scramble to detrain, as it makes only a short stop here. The station platform is very narrow. We get out on the opposite side, onto a wide plaza where a large crowd is waiting. We line up in formation with the teachers upfront.

An elderly dignitary with a red, white, and green sash makes a welcome speech. He speaks perfect German with a Swabian accent. Our director, now camp leader, replies. The Pflegeeltern (foster parents) are arranged corresponding to our groups. Easy, fast matching.

I am introduced to my new family. I will live with Frau Dr. Peter. We meet the foster parents. A smiling, middle-sized man with a trim moustache holds out his hand.

"Sebastian Wittman and my daughter, Marion. My wife, Magda, is at home preparing a welcoming snack."

"Dr. Ilse Peter."

They shake hands.

"And this large rascal is Fredi, Alfred Penz."

I think a little bow is in order and shake Herr Wittman's hand. "Pleased to meet you, Herr Wittman."

"Now, now, no more of that Herr Wittman! From now on, call me Bastibáczi—Uncle Báczi, in Hungarian."

Marion, my new foster sister gives me a hug. I already think I am going to like her. A young fellow in work clothes joins us.

"Frau Doctor, Fredi, this is Janos. He works for us."

"Good afternoon, Janos."

Marion asks, "Fredi, can you say good afternoon, in Hungarian? Jó napot Janos."

"Jó napot Janos, and Servus Janos, in Viennese."

Laughter. Szervusz is hello, in Hungarian, I learn.

The area behind the square is filled with a large variety of horse carriages, foster parents, boys, and teachers. The Wittman's carriage is open with a driver's bench for two and two lengthwise seats in the back. Dr. Peter sits in front with Bastibáczi. Marion, Janos, and I are in the back with the luggage. We travel along one of the main streets that divide Elék.

"This is the centre of town, where the shops, the town hall, the police station, and the town administration are. We, the Germans, are in the majority here, over 70%. There is a large number of Hungarians, some Romanians, and a settlement of Romas (Gypsies) on the outskirts of town. We do not mix with the other nationalities except for work. The centre has electricity, but we on the outskirts do not. They just have not gotten to us yet."

The road is muddy, bumpy, and unpaved with boardwalks to the side. Large farms have huge pens teeming with curly-haired pigs and beam-operated wells. We are on the Puszta, the Hungarian plains.

We drive up to the entrance of a sprawling complex of one-story buildings. A smiling woman with arms wide-open stands in front of the door.

"Welcome to my home."

"Thank you so much for having us, Frau Wittman."

"Now. Do not call me Frau Wittman, Fredi. Call me Magda Néni (Aunt Magda)."

Introductions, round two.

"Dr. Peter, this is Magda, my wife."

"Please, come in. Come in."

We pass a vestibule and enter the largest kitchen/dining room I have ever seen. An oblong oak table that could seat fifteen and a wood-fired oven with a built-in water heater like my grandmother used to have in the early 1930s dominate.

"I am sure you would like to wash up a bit after all that dusty travel. Janos and Pépi (another farmhand) have taken your luggage to your rooms already."

I have a nice room all to myself. There is a beautiful antique armoire and matching chest, both hand-carved and decorated with a painted flower motif that would do any folk museum proud. The bed with its feather duvet looks inviting. I have a washstand with a pitcher, a small desk with a kerosene lamp, and a chamber pot under my bed. The small windows accentuate the thickness of the walls.

Dr. Peter's room is even more impressive. It was Magda's mother's room. The painted folk art furniture is gorgeous. She has more space, a larger desk, and two kerosene lamps. The pitcher on the washstand is a beautiful antique. We are called for dinner. The table is filled with paradise. Butter! White, fresh-baked bread, sausage, pork, bacon, apples, cookies, and a cake. I am definitely going to like it here!

After dinner, Dr. Peter and I are given small flashlights. We are shown the toilet facilities—an outhouse. As outhouses go, it is a nice, roomy one. Before they got English toilets in 1932, my grandparents had a similar arrangement except that it was indoors with a straight chute down to the sewers and cut-up newspapers hung on a nail next to the hole. At this one, you can observe the results and smell them. No newspapers.

"I will also show you how the well works. It is a dip well. This long beam on a pivot has a counterweight on the other end which makes it a lot easier to lift and lower the heavy bucket. We are extremely careful not to contaminate the well. The groundwater level is sometimes very low."

"Fredi, there are few rules here. If you want something, ask for it. When you go out, tell us when you will be back. Do not stray into the other districts; they are pretty well delineated. Be punctual for dinner."

I sleep very well. The polka-dotted duvet's downy feathers are snuggly cozy. Curling in the warmth, I am soon in Morpheus' arms.

I wake to the sounds of a working farm. Not one but three or four roosters cocka-doodle-do-ing.

Are they chasing the hens around?

I go to the washstand, splash some water on my face, and get dressed. The kitchen is full of people.

"Good morning, Fredi. Did you sleep well?"

"I did. I was really tired last night."

The fresh bread, heavily smeared with homemade apricot jam, goes well with a large mug of chicory coffee.

"We are self-sufficient, except for all the stuff we used to get from overseas, such as coffee beans and oranges."

Dr. Peter says, "It will be several days until we can get a school area set up. Your friend, Otto, lives at a farm nearby. Marion has volunteered to take you to where he lives."

"It is just two houses away!"

Splendid idea. We approach a building very similar to the Wittman's.

"Frau Kruger, this is Fredi. He lives with us now."

"Nice to meet you, Frau Kruger."

Otto appears behind her. "Servus Fredi."

"Otto, this is Marion, my foster sister."

"Hi, Otto. Are you Fredi's younger brother? You are quite a bit shorter than Fredi and not as good-looking."

"Do not listen to her, Otto. She is just buttering me up."

Tooot, tooot, tooot, tooot

"What is that tooting? Sounds a bit like a foghorn."

"Oh, that is the pig herder returning the pigs from our communal pastures. If you go quickly, you can see the ritual of our pigs coming home. Go see what is happening!"

Janos and Marion scurry to open the pig pens, and there are a lot of pig pens.

Tooot, tooot, tooot, tooot

Again, the eery foghorn-like sound. Then, voila. The pig herder could be an image straight out of a nineteenth century genre painting. His biblical-looking horn emits a sound that will soon part this sea of pigs. Nonchalantly, he leans on a staff, sporting a waxed moustache—an extra-long, twirled-into-spikes one—that protrudes six inches from each side of his face. His leather vest is adorned with embroidery. He sports plunderpants and high leather boots and has his all-weather cape flung back in a regal pose. Behind and around him is an ocean of bobbing black fur. Hundreds and hundreds of black, curly-haired pigs of all sizes. Then, miraculously, this huge sea parts into groups, each group heading for their home pen. Tasty corn awaits for supper.

The next day, Marion takes us to the town centre where all the shops and major buildings are. Reaching the commercial section, we are mesmerized by the display of plenty in the shop windows.

"Look at the suits and coats, five thousand Pengö. How much is that in Reichsmark?"

"Do not look at it, boys. Inflation. Far too much even for us."

"Look at these boots."

Everyone in Elék seems to sport boots, heavy army boots or elegant riding ones. Our footwear is worn. Going along the row of boots on display, we give each pair an imaginary owner. This pair for a peasant, this for a shopkeeper, this for an officer, and that pair for Count Esterházy.

"Do not worry, Fredi. Mother will find you an old pair of rubber boots for when the rainy season starts."

And then there is the candy store, all kinds of candy.

"Marion, can you lend us a few Heller until we get our first allowance?"

We merrily suck on candy.

"Mine is strawberry."

"Mine is orange."

There has not been any candy in Vienna for years.

We saunter past the government buildings, the police station, and the administrative building and sit for a while on a bench in a small park.

"It is sometimes a bit boring here. We had a cinema, but it stopped three months ago. I remember German films synchronized into Hungarian, with Romanian subtitles. I remember Hans Moser talking to Heinz Rühmann in Hungarian. He did not even mumble in Hungarian."

"You are over sixteen, Marion. Do you go to any dances?"

"There are none. We dance at most weddings—when there are any—but most of the young men are at the front. Far too many are dead. The war has killed so many of them. My parents used to take me to Békéscaba sometimes, to see a film or go to the baths. They have nifty baths in Békéscaba. Do you know how to swim, Fredi?"

"Yes, of course. We swim in the Old Danube, a side branch of the river. It is really great."

We have our first Hitler Youth assembly. The camp leader has decided that we should keep a low profile. The great majority of Germans here are not National Socialists. Siegfried Wessely, our physical education teacher is in charge. He has found a way to combine physical education with the obligatory assembly.

We have the use of a soccer field with a gravel foundation and sod cover. The locals have stopped playing, as most of the players are at the front. We march in formation, do our army-style drills, run around the field, and do callisthenics.

Sometimes the camp leader takes command. He appears in his Air Defence uniform topped by a strange helmet. Air Defence is just one of the fifty-odd National Socialist organizations, each with its own ranks, uniforms, and special medals. He was in the First World War and sometimes confuses the old commands with the German ones, such “Habt Acht!” for “Stillgestanden!” and so on. His face is horribly disfigured, not from the war, but from when one of his chemistry experiments exploded in his face. He is the only party member among the teachers.

I am learning to read and study by the light of a kerosene lamp. It is a bit hard on the eyes, especially when reading small type, but I guess you adapt.

Our first day back in class. Quite a large room with small makeshift desks without drawers. There is no teacher’s podium. Dr. Trnka, our history teacher, sits in the middle of us. He gives us an overview of Hungary’s past. Dr. Trnka’s teaching method is exceptional. No reciting boring names and dates. A perfect storyteller, he has the gift of conjuring up the past. Details, interrelations, personalities. History with him beats going to the movies.

Otto and I are learning to play a Hungarian snake and ladders game with Marion and her friend, Anushka. All the instructions are in Hungarian. We accuse the girls of cheating.

“Look,” we say, pointing to an instruction. “This says go 15 numbers backward, not forward.”

The girls try to teach us the Hungarian ditty, Poros, poros, az Elekí utca. ‘It is dusty. It is dusty on Elék’s streets.’ A beautiful Eléki woman will smear jam on my face, and a beautiful young girl will lick it off.

You will not smear any jam on my face! In my mouth, maybe, but definitely not my face.

I am better at singing this ditty than Otto.

School is what school always is, maybe a bit more interesting. Our relationships with the teachers are more intimate. We are more of a team. School-wise, I am faring better here.

There is still some time left for mischief though. One of our main targets is the train station. Sometimes it is just a place to hang out, to watch passengers arrive or depart, but a major attraction is the toilets. It is so nice to sit on a porcelain throne instead of a board with a hole in it. How clever of the English. Just pull the chain and it flushes.

“Have you ever gone on the ladies’ toilet?”

“I dare you!”

A figure appears. An angry little man in uniform points at the sign on the door and then beats on it like a kettledrum.

“NÖK! “NÖK! “NÖK!” In a more informative tone, he points at the other sign. “FÉRFIAK! FÉRFIAK!”

“Igén, inspektor, Igén!”

With little bows like nice little Viennese boys, we slink off.

NÖK! “NÖK! What a good name for that guy. Of course, we already knew that Férfiak means men. We stay away from the station for a while.

Tak, tak, takTak tak, tak, tak tak… tak

Is that small arms fire?

“Fredi, do not worry about the shooting. The Hungarian Army has their regular manoeuvres this time of year.”

“So close to the Romanian border?”

“Well, I think that is why the Romanians do it at the same time. The Hungarians and the Romanians traditionally hate each other, even if they fight and die side-by-side on the Russian front. Each country maintains a whole division at the common border.”

“It is mainly about Transylvania, Siebenbürgen, as you know it.”

Tak, tak, tak, tak, tak, tak, tak.
tak, tak, tak, tak

A soldier pops up among the pigs in one of the pens. The pigs seem unperturbed. They have been through this before. Swine are sometimes smarter than we are; they have a remarkable memory.

Out on the road, a bicycle troop detail in green uniforms and

Darby hats adorned with rooster tails pedal along the wooden boardwalk. At a whistle, the whole lot dives onto the muddy road.

Tak, tak, tak, tak,..
tak, tak, tak, tak…Tak, tak, tak, tak, tak

A splendid hussar splashes through the mud at full gallop. His horse rears. There is the glitter of a golden trumpet.

Tatatatateraa, tatatatateraa.
The manoeuvres are over.

Downtown, later that day, there are a lot of soldiers—some in formation, some mounted on trucks. And then, a tableau straight out of the Emperor's time, a six-wheeled open command vehicle. Several high-ranking officers are in the vehicle; the commander, a colonel sits on the back row.

Everyone is smartly turned out in the high Kepi of the old Imperial Army and immaculate riding boots. The colonel is in light blue, monocled, with an Emperor Francis Josef beard. A group of five officers, one by one, step up to report. A click of the heels, a salute, a slight almost Viennese bow.

"Major Janos Nagy, begs to report to your excellency."

This must be the stinkiest day of my young life. Janos and a guy from our swine squad are emptying the outhouse of its contents. They are dressed for the occasion: rubber boots, long-sleeved rubber gloves, and rubber aprons. For the duration of the task, all of our defecations are to be in a chamber pot.

They have already dismantled the outhouse proper. It ingeniously comes apart and is set aside. A large two-wheeled, zinc-lined cart called the honey wagon receives the feces, which are scooped into it with a long-handled tool. The full cart is then pushed and pulled to the garden where its contents are spread around the vegetable beds as fertilizer. Back and forth, this goes on all day. They are not even wearing gas masks!

"Marion, can you blow my nose, please?" He explains, "The more you work with nature, the more you get used to it."

Contact with my parents is a problem. The mail to and from Vienna takes between two and three weeks. About a hundred men from town have volunteered to serve in the German SS to avoid the Hungarian draft. Some of them post the odd letter for us in Germany on their way to and from the front.

Speaking of mail, I must admit to my young life's first unlawful act. The Hungarian tobacco authority holds a monopoly on matches and forbids the use of cigarette lighters. Many Hungarians do own lighters, though, for which fuel is no problem but flints are. All of our regular mail appears with a big fat 'CENSURED' stamp on it, ensuring that its contents have been checked. In a letter sent via the SS, I ask my mother to bake me a cake with a package of flints baked inside it and to send it via regular mail. She does—a little cake with a hundred flints baked inside. Janos sells them, a little pocket money for him and me.

Otto asked me once if I get homesick. I do, for my parents and Aunt Ria. I am still a proud Viennese boy, but I sure am enjoying this prolonged vacation.

The days are getting shorter. The rainy season begins with mud and cold. The news from the front is disastrous. The entire Hungarian Sixth Army was annihilated. The Romanians and the Italians are not faring any better. Not having enough anti-tank weapons, they are overrun by highly mobile Siberian troops. Newly equipped with thousands of American tanks and trucks, re-armed and re-trained, they emerged from behind the Ural Mountains. The entire German Sixth Army is encircled in Stalingrad. Magda's nephew has been killed. The family is despondent. Many more casualties are expected. Elék is gloomy these days. A pall of pending defeat hangs over us, adding a touch of anxiety to our lives.

Most of the town has no refrigeration. To overcome this, they have a fully equipped communal abattoir (slaughterhouse). Each of the farmers in the arrangement has a particular week to butcher. By distributing fresh cuts and sausages among themselves, everyone has fresh meat during the winter and smoked meat during summer.

"Fredi, do you want to come along?"

"Of course, I do."

It is also a social occasion. Everyone has a couple of glasses of wine, but for me, it is apple juice. And then precise teamwork. Josef brings in the victim, a large curly-haired black boar. It sniffles, sensing that something untoward is going to happen. A stun gun is pressed against the head. Bang. A bolt shoots into the cranium. A knife slices the throat. A white basin is shoved under the head. The gushing red blood is collected, to be turned into blood sausage later. A few slight quivers and the pig is dead. A couple of cuts in the ankles and the beast hangs on butcher hooks to be dissected into cuts of which any professional butcher would approve.

Large bowls file down the line with chunks of pork, ingredients for sausage, head cheese, and pork hocks. Intestines are cleaned and treated to become sausage casings. The abattoir is equipped with hand-cranked sausage-making machines and a large smokehouse with partitions for each farmer. Everything they need to produce at the quality of city butchers.

Otto and I go for a stroll, just sauntering about and, as they would accuse, looking for mischief, although it is not always for mischief. The sun is shining. What a beautiful day. The flatness of the Puszta landscape defines the sky as a straight line.

"Does it not seem to you that there is more sky here than at home?"

"Ja, at home the hills are in the way."

The sun composes the colours of the arid, flat land into a palette of matte greens and ochres. Specs of light glitter on the pale blue flat ponds.

"Looks romantic, makes you feel poetic."

"Have you ever tried a verse ending with Hitler? Hitler, bittler."

"Stop it!"

"Look at those clouds! Some of them look like objects, I think. Like monsters, ghosts."

The sky is scattered with cirrus clouds.

"Does this not remind you of the torn cotton candy we got at the Prater?"

The Prater, there is no amusement park like it.

"What is your favourite at the Prater?"

"Definitely the giant roller coaster!"

"Ja, that is great. The spooky ghost train, the panorama train, and the water splash rides are not bad either."

"It is all fun. I remember when I would not get out of the bumper car."

"Do you think it is still working during the war?"

"Do you think we ever will be confirmed? You know, the whole schmier with a gold watch and ride in a Fiacre (small carriage) to the Prater afterward?"

"Well, after the war there will not be any men left to be sponsors and definitely no gold watches."

"Heaven only knows what they are doing."

"Fredi, I have been thinking about Dr. Trnka's lecture about battles in the past, about the mercenaries lying mutilated on the fields, about their women who travelled in wagons behind the army looking for them, and troops marching towards death in formation, as in so many wars previously. What it would be like to be shot at, to be hit. Or to be on the front. To kill people."

"If you had an enemy in your sights, what would you aim for to bring him down without killing him?"

"Well, certainly not the abdomen. That would destroy several major organs. The stomach and the intestines would cause a horribly painful death."

"Maybe the right shoulder away from the heart?"

"Maybe just shoot off their willie?"

"Let's get off this subject. It is creepy, especially since sooner or later we might be targets."

"Ja, the bombing bit is bad enough."

Do not think about it. Whenever you think about any of that, it paralyzes you. What happens, happens. You have to accept it.

"Do you think the war will last long enough for us to be drafted into the army?"

The abattoir is not the only communal institution. There is also a distillery. Every farmer in the concern has his day at the still.

"Fredi, do you want to watch how we make our Schnapps?"

I join Janos, Pépi, and another fellow I do not know. They are busy loading what they call the ladder carriage. Barrels of vile-smelling goop, the fermented peels and skins of pressed grapes.

I sit on the front bench with Janos, who guides the horse. I love horses. There were five at the farm. We arrive at a massive stone building. Entering, we face a humongous apparatus. A monster-sized metal boiler with pipes going in and around it. When everything is unloaded, the preparations start.

A raging fire needs to be lit to provide enough heat to extract the alcohol from the goop. It will take quite a while to get the still working. The outcome will be a spirit not unlike Italian grappa. Janos has taken the horse and wagon back to the farm.

Now it is time to sit around and wait. Talking, drinking beer, and munching on our brought-along victuals—bread, homemade cheese, and sausages. The boys tease me, goading me into trying what is dripping out of a small spout on the side of the still. As the hours pass, the mood becomes more animated.

"You Viennese, hupp, cannot drink."

"I bet you cannot drink this cup in one gulp!"

I feel the heat of the foul, reeking potion in my throat, then the lights go out.

Oh God, my head. My gut is exploding.

When I wake up fully, I am lying on my bed, half undressed. There is a bucket. I retch, retch, retch. My head is spinning. My mouth feels as if the Russian Army has marched through it.

I had passed out at the still. After being slumped in a corner for several hours like a rag doll, they loaded me into a wheelbarrow and meandered home, losing me in the mud and finding me again. Arriving at the house, they had cleaned the worst off of me and deposited me on my bed.

It took the combined hangover recipes and intense mothering of Magda and Dr. Peter to get me back to normal. The boys got a severe dressing down. Miraculously, I was not punished. This was my first experience with the spirit demon.

The first snow. Winter is here.

Otto has to check with Ferenc Szabó, the tailor, about an order. Having nothing else to do, I trundle along. The Szabó house has a fenced-in yard. To see if anyone might be at the back of the house, we enter the yard. Instantly, we are attacked by a vicious, ill-tempered little creature called Churchill (pronounced Khurkhill), a very aggressive, ugly bull terrier.

"Careful, he bites!"

The dog's teeth clench onto my trouser leg. Otto kicks him loose. There is lovely wet, fresh snow all around. Soon the beastie is under rapid snowball fire. He races round and round the yard trying to avoid the hard snowballs. In despair, he seeks refuge in the partly open outhouse. After cowering first in a bottom corner, he jumps up onto the seat. The snowballs still come. Then, scratch, scratch, scratch…

My God, he is gone. Holy shit. He is down the hole. There he is, whimpering and half submerged in a sea of feces.

"He is high enough. Should we try to get him out?"

"No, the shit is pretty solid. Let's clean up the snow and get the hell out of here."

What are they are going to do to us? Will anyone believe we did not throw him in? They cannot extradite us, but can they expel us from school?

Fortunately, it snows later which covers up our tracks. At least the dog's name was not Hitler. For three days, the tension gets worse and worse, some of the worst in my young life.

On the fourth day, Marion, sitting at the table says, "I heard the strangest story. You know Szabó, the tailor that has a little bull terrier called Churchill? Well, when he came home late a few days ago, he could not find his dog. After a while, he had to go to the toilet, but when he sat down he heard the dog whimpering below in the feces! He was able to lift the dog out by its collar, but it got loose and headed straight into the parlour scraping feces off on its way. It had snowed quite heavily that night and got very cold. The dog must have looked for shelter."

Oh, what a relief it is.

There is a long railway track that leads to Lökösháza and beyond to the border. It is a single track with maybe one train a day in each direction. The track's embankment passes along a stretch of shallow wetlands, now frozen over. Otto and I are walking on the sleepers, picking up pebbles from the rail bed. A telegraph line runs along the tracks.

"I bet you cannot hit one of the wires and make it sing."

It takes a lot of skill to hit a wire.

"Oh God, look. There is a guy with a big stick running towards us on the track."

"Hell, it is Nök, the station master!"

"Run, Otto! Run!"

"He is gaining on us fast."

"Quick, onto the ice!"

"Are you crazy?"

"It is the only way!"

We slide down onto the ice. It cracks under our feet. We do not break through. Nök is so close behind that we can almost feel his grip on our necks.

Crash, crash, crash, crash

Then, a horrible Hungarian curse. He has broken through the ice.

This must be the stinkiest day of my young life. Janos and a guy from our swine squad are emptying the outhouse of its contents. They are dressed for the occasion: rubber boots, long-sleeved rubber gloves, and rubber aprons. For the duration of the task, all of our defecations are to be in a chamber pot.

They have already dismantled the outhouse proper. It ingeniously comes apart and is set aside. A large two-wheeled, zinc-lined cart called the honey wagon receives the feces, which are scooped into it with a long-handled tool. The full cart is then pushed and pulled to the garden where its contents are spread around the vegetable beds as fertilizer. Back and forth, this goes on all day. They are not even wearing gas masks!

"Marion, can you blow my nose, please?" He explains, "The more you work with nature, the more you get used to it."

Contact with my parents is a problem. The mail to and from Vienna takes between two and three weeks. About a hundred men from town have volunteered to serve in the German SS to avoid the Hungarian draft. Some of them post the odd letter for us in Germany on their way to and from the front.

Speaking of mail, I must admit to my young life's first unlawful act. The Hungarian tobacco authority holds a monopoly on matches and forbids the use of cigarette lighters. Many Hungarians do own lighters, though, for which fuel is no problem but flints are. All of our regular mail appears with a big fat 'CENSURED' stamp on it, ensuring that its contents have been checked. In a letter sent via the SS, I ask my mother to bake me a cake with a package of flints baked inside it and to send it via regular mail. She does—a little cake with a hundred flints baked inside. Janos sells them, a little pocket money for him and me.

Otto asked me once if I get homesick. I do, for my parents and Aunt Ria. I am still a proud Viennese boy, but I sure am enjoying this prolonged vacation.

The days are getting shorter. The rainy season begins with mud and cold. The news from the front is disastrous. The entire Hungarian Sixth Army was annihilated. The Romanians and the Italians are not faring any better. Not having enough anti-tank weapons, they are overrun by highly mobile Siberian troops. Newly equipped with thousands of American tanks and trucks, re-armed and re-trained, they emerged from behind the Ural Mountains. The entire German Sixth Army is encircled in Stalingrad. Magda's nephew has been killed. The family is despondent. Many more casualties are expected. Elék is gloomy these days. A pall of pending defeat hangs over us, adding a touch of anxiety to our lives.

Most of the town has no refrigeration. To overcome this, they have a fully equipped communal abattoir (slaughterhouse). Each of the farmers in the arrangement has a particular week to butcher. By distributing fresh cuts and sausages among themselves, everyone has fresh meat during the winter and smoked meat during summer.

"Fredi, do you want to come along?"

"Of course, I do."

It is also a social occasion. Everyone has a couple of glasses of wine, but for me, it is apple juice. And then precise teamwork. Josef brings in the victim, a large curly-haired black boar. It sniffles, sensing that something untoward is going to happen. A stun gun is pressed against the head. Bang. A bolt shoots into the cranium. A knife slices the throat. A white basin is shoved under the head. The gushing red blood is collected, to be turned into blood sausage later. A few slight quivers and the pig is dead. A couple of cuts in the ankles and the beast hangs on butcher hooks to be dissected into cuts of which any professional butcher would approve.

Large bowls file down the line with chunks of pork, ingredients for sausage, head cheese, and pork hocks. Intestines are cleaned and treated to become sausage casings. The abattoir is equipped with hand-cranked sausage-making machines and a large smokehouse with partitions for each farmer. Everything they need to produce at the quality of city butchers.

. . .

Otto and I go for a stroll, just sauntering about and, as they would accuse, looking for mischief, although it is not always for mischief. The sun is shining. What a beautiful day. The flatness of the Puszta landscape defines the sky as a straight line.

"Does it not seem to you that there is more sky here than at home?"

"Ja, at home the hills are in the way."

The sun composes the colours of the arid, flat land into a palette of matte greens and ochres. Specs of light glitter on the pale blue flat ponds.

"Looks romantic, makes you feel poetic."

"Have you ever tried a verse ending with Hitler? Hitler, bittler."

"Stop it!"

"Look at those clouds! Some of them look like objects, I think. Like monsters, ghosts."

The sky is scattered with cirrus clouds.

"Does this not remind you of the torn cotton candy we got at the Prater?"

The Prater, there is no amusement park like it.

"What is your favourite at the Prater?"

"Definitely the giant roller coaster!"

"Ja, that is great. The spooky ghost train, the panorama train, and the water splash rides are not bad either."

"It is all fun. I remember when I would not get out of the bumper car."

"Do you think it is still working during the war?"

"Do you think we ever will be confirmed? You know, the whole schmier with a gold watch and ride in a Fiacre (small carriage) to the Prater afterward?"

"Well, after the war there will not be any men left to be sponsors and definitely no gold watches."

"Heaven only knows what they are doing."

"Fredi, I have been thinking about Dr. Trnka's lecture about battles in the past, about the mercenaries lying mutilated on the fields, about their women who travelled in wagons behind the army looking for them, and troops marching towards death in formation, as in so many wars previously. What it would be like to be shot at, to be hit. Or to be on the front. To kill people."

"If you had an enemy in your sights, what would you aim for to bring him down without killing him?"

"Well, certainly not the abdomen. That would destroy several major organs. The stomach and the intestines would cause a horribly painful death."

"Maybe the right shoulder away from the heart?"

"Maybe just shoot off their willie?"

"Let's get off this subject. It is creepy, especially since sooner or later we might be targets."

"Ja, the bombing bit is bad enough."

Do not think about it. Whenever you think about any of that, it paralyzes you. What happens, happens. You have to accept it.

"Do you think the war will last long enough for us to be drafted into the army?"

The abattoir is not the only communal institution. There is also a distillery. Every farmer in the concern has his day at the still.

"Fredi, do you want to watch how we make our Schnapps?"

I join Janos, Pépi, and another fellow I do not know. They are busy loading what they call the ladder carriage. Barrels of vile-smelling goop, the fermented peels and skins of pressed grapes.

I sit on the front bench with Janos, who guides the horse. I love horses. There were five at the farm. We arrive at a massive stone building. Entering, we face a humongous apparatus. A monster-sized metal boiler with pipes going in and around it. When everything is unloaded, the preparations start.

A raging fire needs to be lit to provide enough heat to extract the alcohol from the goop. It will take quite a while to get the still working. The outcome will be a spirit not unlike Italian grappa. Janos has taken the horse and wagon back to the farm.

Now it is time to sit around and wait. Talking, drinking beer, and munching on our brought-along victuals—bread, homemade cheese, and sausages. The boys tease me, goading me into trying what is dripping out of a small spout on the side of the still. As the hours pass, the mood becomes more animated.

"You Viennese, hupp, cannot drink."

"I bet you cannot drink this cup in one gulp!"

I feel the heat of the foul, reeking potion in my throat, then the lights go out.

Oh God, my head. My gut is exploding.

When I wake up fully, I am lying on my bed, half undressed.

There is a bucket. I retch, retch, retch. My head is spinning. My mouth feels as if the Russian Army has marched through it.

I had passed out at the still. After being slumped in a corner for several hours like a rag doll, they loaded me into a wheelbarrow and meandered home, losing me in the mud and finding me again. Arriving at the house, they had cleaned the worst off of me and deposited me

on my bed.

It took the combined hangover recipes and intense mothering of Magda and Dr. Peter to get me back to normal. The boys got a severe dressing down. Miraculously, I was not punished. This was my first experience with the spirit demon.

The first snow. Winter is here.

Otto has to check with Ferenc Szabó, the tailor, about an order. Having nothing else to do, I trundle along. The Szabó house has a fenced-in yard. To see if anyone might be at the back of the house, we enter the yard. Instantly, we are attacked by a vicious, ill-tempered little creature called Churchill (pronounced Khurkhill), a very aggressive, ugly bull terrier.

"Careful, he bites!"

The dog's teeth clench onto my trouser leg. Otto kicks him loose. There is lovely wet, fresh snow all around. Soon the beastie is under rapid snowball fire. He races round and round the yard trying to avoid the hard snowballs. In despair, he seeks refuge in the partly open outhouse. After cowering first in a bottom corner, he jumps up onto the seat. The snowballs still come. Then, scratch, scratch, scratch…

My God, he is gone. Holy shit. He is down the hole. There he is, whimpering and half submerged in a sea of feces.

"He is high enough. Should we try to get him out?"

"No, the shit is pretty solid. Let's clean up the snow and get the hell out of here."

What are they are going to do to us? Will anyone believe we did not throw him in? They cannot extradite us, but can they expel us from school?

Fortunately, it snows later which covers up our tracks. At least the dog's name was not Hitler. For three days, the tension gets worse and worse, some of the worst in my young life.

On the fourth day, Marion, sitting at the table says, "I heard the strangest story. You know Szabó, the tailor that has a little bull terrier called Churchill? Well, when he came home late a few days ago, he could not find his dog. After a while, he had to go to the toilet, but when he sat down he heard the dog whimpering below in the feces! He was able to lift the dog out by its collar, but it got loose and headed straight into the parlour scraping feces off on its way. It had snowed quite heavily that night and got very cold. The dog must have looked for shelter."

Oh, what a relief it is.

Christmas, the Teutonic festival of light or the birth of Jesus.

We are assembled at the Lutheran church hall. Since there is not a single coniferous tree for kilometres, a large swastika flag has to do. The camp leader holds a speech.

"We thank the Führer for having brought us here and protecting us." Not a word about peace and goodwill to all, just the usual rambling about efforts to reach victory. "We shall prevail, and at the end, we shall be united with our families. The Führer has provided a little gift for each of you, so Merry Christmas and Heil Hitler."

Every boy is given a small bag of candy and a Reichspost certificate for five Reichsmark.

Can I convert that into Pengös? Has the Führer run out of money?

Back at the Wittman's, Christmas is very different. Many delicious aromas welcome us—Magda's temple of culinary art. I am sent to wait in my room. A glass of cider and some pickles and onions are on my desk. When I am called, I see a Christmas Wonderland.

"Frohe Weihnachten (Merry Christmas), Fredi."

Around twenty candles in decoratively carved holders conjure up a special feeling. Christmas, the festival of lights. We take our places around the table. I sit between Marion and Dr. Peter. Bastibáczi stands up.

"You know that we are Lutheran, so I shall say the Christmas grace in Hungarian."

Dr. Peter says the Catholic version in Latin.

Peace on Earth.

The first course appears—a gorgeous fish on a platter. Bastibáczi does the honours and carves the fish.

"You know, like you in Austria, we breed our carp in special ponds, usually with a pike added to chase them a bit so they do not become too fat. Just before Christmas, we pull the pond's plug and the carp land on our table."

Magda brings out the next course. Too bad we do not have an orchestra playing the triumphal march from Aida. Roast goose, galuskas (dumplings), and red cabbage. Heavenly, goose crackling, galuskas that melt in your mouth. And to top it off, rétes (apple strudel). A meal to propel a boy who lived on 50g of meat from coupon five of the ration card back home into sixth heaven, maybe seventh if there is such a thing.

And then the presents—a pair of warm socks, one foot knitted by Magda, the other by Marion, and from Dr. Peter, a book by Franz Werfel.

"Do not show it to anyone. It is banned in Germany. They burn it. It is alright with the Hungarians, though, they have not burned any books yet."

Dr. Peter has adopted me. She is very kind. She helps me with my school work and talks to me. She also lets me stay when she has conversations with the foster parents. She says one can talk freely here, without informants lurking to turn you in. Unfortunately, the events outside of Elék do not make for good conversation. There are leisurely evening talks and sometimes Magda and Marion take part.

The topic this evening is the catastrophe at Stalingrad. The whole of the German Sixth Army is trapped. The whole of the Hungarian First Army, the Romanian Sixth Army, and six hundred thousand Italians have been annihilated by fresh Russian troops, trained and superbly equipped behind the Ural Mountains where German Intelligence could not detect them. The situation reminds Bastibáczi of the first few months of the First World War.

"I was a Honvéd sergeant at the time. Archduke Albert and his cronies were having parties instead of leading the army. I barely got out of the Siege of Przemyšl."

"I know, Sebastian. I lost my husband during the same period. He was a lieutenant with the Kaiserjägers. He fell in Russia. Their commander did not send scouts ahead and led them into an ambush decimating the regiment."

"Does that not remind you of our glorious leaders at this stage of the war? We do not know what the future holds for us. We Hungarian Germans were better off under the monarchy which settled us here in the first place. But since Austria was not a country then, only the inherited domain of the Habsburg family, things got muddled after the breakup of the monarchy.

"What happened during the post-war period under Béla Kun, the communist, was horrible. They confiscated much of our private property. But then Miklós Horthy drove them out with the help of the Romanians. Thankfully, despite all the governmental changes, nobody was directly anti-German. We were just another minority. But this time it is different, and I am very afraid."

News is slow to reach our house. Since we have no electricity, there is no telephone or radio. Bastibáczi's friend Thomas comes to the house very agitated.

"The Romanians have capitulated."

Are they going to change sides?

The Hungarian-refurbished First Army and the Romanian Fourth Army have been decimated at the Carpathian passes. The Russian Army under Malenkow is pushing rapidly towards us. It all happens so suddenly. This means goodbye to our Hungarian home. We are told one day and have to leave the next. We gather our things. Martha packs some provisions for us. Bastibáczi drives us to the station. The sights of Elék pass by at a slow trot for the last time.

They tell us Hitler Youth do not cry, but we have a hard time holding back our tears.

They are all there at the platform—Bastibáczi, Magda, Marion, Anushka, Janos, and all our friends. They are all crying for us and for themselves.

As the train starts moving, everyone calls, "Auf Wiedersehen. Viszontlátásra. Ishten legyen veled (God be with you)."

I ask Otto, "Do you think Adam and Eve were crying?"

A NARROW ESCAPE FROM THE VOJVODINA

We are to stay with Ethnic Germans in a small Serbian town in the Vojvodina, or Basca as the Hungarians call it, about fifteen kilometres south of Subotica. The railway is clear up to Szeged, where we stop on a siding and are passed by long troop trains going south. Another army on the move.

Arriving in town, we are awaited by a large, rather formal group. I will again stay with Dr. Peter. Our new hosts are Herr Josef Neubauer and his wife, Maria. Herr Neubauer is as tall as my father. He and she are in their fifties. We climb into their Steyr automobile. Arriving at their house, we are pleasantly surprised. It is very modern.

"Welcome to our home."

There is electricity and the interior is very elegant. Herr Neubauer is a real estate agent. They have one son, who serves on the Eastern Front.

We are led to our very comfortable and spacious rooms. Modern furniture, washbasins with running water, and hurray, a bathtub with separate shower. Dr. Peter even has an ensuite English toilet. She lets me flush it. There is an elegant dining room where we sit down for Kaiserbuns, two kinds of jam, and ersatz coffee or herbal tea.

It is agreed that Dr. Peter and the Neumanns will address themselves by their first names. I shall call them Herr and Frau Neumann, like I would back home in Vienna. I sleep well in a bed with flannel sheets, cozy blankets, and a spring mattress.

The next morning, after a breakfast of rye bread with butter and jam and coffee, I set out to explore the town. It looks like any other small German town in Franconia or Thuringia—neat, clean, and proper, with cobblestone pavement throughout. There is an onion-domed church, arched passageways, and small pubs with German signs. I know Otto is in one of these houses. I just do not know which one. I will have to wait until school starts to see him. It takes about a week for our first school day.

One evening, while Dr. Peter, the Neumanns, and I sit together, Herr Neumann says to Dr. Peter, "I am surprised, given the precarious military situation, that your government did not repatriate your group directly to Germany, while it can still be done without any serious danger. In 1941, after Germany defeated the Royal Yugoslavian Army, Hungary invaded all the territories it lost at the Treaty of Trianon. They killed about three thousand Serbians at Novi Sad, or Neusatz as we call it.

"In the tit for tat politics of this region, they now lump Germans with the Hungarians, especially after the Germans in the Banat formed a regional German government. Not to mention the fascist Croatians, the Ustaše. Life was not bad under the Yugoslavian kings. We minded our own business and they left us alone. We even went on holiday to Montenegro and Venice. Now we only have our worthless Yugoslavian passports. Where can we escape to and in which direction? Should we abandon everything we own and leave our old and infirm behind?"

Dr. Peter is very pensive these days.

"Have faith, Fredi. Have faith."

Our time here only lasts fourteen days, just as we have settled into a regular school routine.

"There has been a Chetnik attack only 15km from here. Draza Mihailović's boys. Also, a large group of Tito's communists are marching north towards us."

We have to leave and we have to leave fast. The locals conduct a desperate search to find rail transport for us. They are concerned the Russians will cut off our route to Vienna. The farewell to our foster families is not as dramatic as the goodbyes in Elék. We are all too preoccupied by fear. We, about beating the Russians to Vienna, they about their future. It feels like leaving people on death row.

We are on a train moving north. We pass Subotica and the former border. Reaching Szeged, we are shunted onto a sidetrack. Hours pass. One German troop train after another passes us, some going east, some west.

We hear that Admiral Horthy was deposed and taken to Germany. The Arrow Cross leader is now the Hungarian prime minister. The Romanians and the Bulgarians have capitulated and changed sides. They are now fighting us. Horthy was about to do the same.

Finally, we reach Kecskemét. Our conductor tells us that the Soviets are attacking Debrecen. We reach the outskirts of Budapest. The rails around the city are in shambles. We are decoupled and shunted to a siding for another nail-biting wait.

Planes pass above us.

Are they friend or foe?

We are coupled to a train going west. Finally, we are rolling towards home. The countryside looks more and more like Austria. After passing Györ, we stop again on a sidetrack. On one side of us, a long train carries an SS division to the front. Tiger tanks sit on flatbeds and troops in passenger cars.

On the other side sits is a row of cattle cars. A group of Arrow Cross troopers are loading people into them. The doors of the cars are pretty high up. A long row of people are lined up—men, women, and children. The male prisoners help the others up. An old woman cannot quite make it, so the trooper next to her slaps her across the face and kicks her as she falls.

Who are these prisoners? Jews or enemies of the state? I remember my school friend, David Levy. *Whatever happened to him?*

When I was nine or ten, while I was playing with David at his apartment, Frau Levy said, "Fredi, do not come to us anymore."

"But Frau Levy, what have I done?"

"Fredi, my love, you have not done anything. Just do not come anymore."

Three weeks later, the family disappeared.

Just before the border, we are shunted onto a side spur again. This time we are passed by a long train of cattle cars with a single passenger car at the end. Prisoners.

We pass the German border. As we roll into Vienna's Eastern Railway Station, we are welcomed by the wail of air-raid sirens.

We are home.

THE SWOOSH OF THE SCYTHE

3

MY FAMILY LIFE in Vienna is now somewhat complicated. My mother has evacuated to Aigen-Schägl because she is expecting my new sibling and cannot leave the new baby there alone. Now I will have to learn how to be a big brother to a brother or sister.

I do not know much about girls. I have never had a sister or female friends and all my schooling has been in boys-only environments. I do not even know what girls' nether regions look like. My female cousins and I did do some show-and-tell once when we were little during a family party after we were all deposited in the spare room. I admit that I enjoyed that.

As a very small boy, I rarely met other children before kindergarten, except when the extended family met for dinner or went on family visits, such as to my grandmother's brother. He was postal director for the district of Baden and lived in a large villa. I remember sitting with my father's cousins for dinner at the children's table, called the 'cat's table.'

My grandmother's family, the Kschwent family, was very large. They originated from a town north of the Czechoslovakian border and had an estate there. My grandmother had a sister, Poldi, who was the fashion plate of the family. She married a First World War ace fighter pilot. My grandmother and aunt often pampered me.

When I was about six, my father, who was nuts about anything with a motor, bought an Indian 500cc motorcycle with a sidecar. After that, Father, Mother and I, in goggles and leather caps, explored the countryside. I loved those outings, especially the ones ending at little lakes, where I learned to swim and floated on an inflated inner tube.

In the city of Vienna, my grandfather operated a dairy that had been founded in 1827. There were cows and also horses, goats, and pigs on it. It prospered during the depression but was no longer profitable after the German pasteurization laws came into effect in 1938. That year, after the dairy closed, my father decided to have the family's transport license changed from horse transport to motor transport. Then he bought a truck and went into business for himself. He bought a brand new three-ton Opel Blitz, which he collected at the factory in Berlin.

Soon, he had a thriving business going, focused mainly on the vegetable market. After the occupation of Czechoslovakia, the German Army hired Viennese truckers on a day-by-day basis. The German Army was sixty percent horse-drawn at the time and needed trucks. When the war with Poland started, Father was offered the same opportunity and took it, thinking the war would be over in two or three weeks. It was not.

The army confiscated the truck and conscripted him, too. It took him a year to get out of the army. In the meantime, my mother purchased an old three-ton Italian Fiat 626 and hired a driver until Father could get back. The trouble was that it was built for left-hand traffic with the steering wheel on the right-hand side, so it was difficult to drive. Until 1938, Italy, Austria, and all the Eastern European countries had left-hand traffic.

My father does not know how to boil an egg nor is he about to learn. Aunt Ria lives in our building, but unfortunately, she and Father do not get along well—something to do with her and grandmother not accepting Mother after my parents married. But, thankfully, Aunt Ria loves me and gleefully becomes my cooking instructor. She shows me how to make something edible out of our woeful rations.

The ration card provides only enough nutrition for a subsistence existence, so grocery shopping becomes an expedition. Aunt Ria, who has always been very frugal, coaches me on how to cook with what we get. It is hard to cook with only the amounts on the ration card. Without fat, it is difficult to make a proper roux for soups, and we have to be stingy with the flour, too.

I do the grocery shopping in stages, going around the block. I can skip the dairy because milk is only for infants.

STOP ONE: The Dry Goods Grocer

STOP TWO: The Greengrocer

STOP THREE: The Butcher

STOP FOUR: The Baker

Before I start, I find suitable containers—bottles for liquids, paper sacks for dry goods, and for baked goods, the ubiquitous large net bag. The dry goods grocer—such as for flour and noodles—is across the street. The greengrocer is around the corner. The baker is on the opposite corner of that block, and the butcher is around another corner.

At the dry goods grocer, everything is weighted on a mechanical scale with little weights on one side and the food on the other. Items such as flour are scooped out of barrels, noodles out of drawers. Buying only fifty grams of pork, as you can imagine, has its issues. For the elderly and single working people with seventy hour work weeks, shopping poses special problems. How the shops stay in business, I do not know. Aunt Ria insists on doing her own shopping, it gets her out of the house and lets her catch up on the latest gossip.

We have no refrigeration since the iceman does not come anymore. He used to bring us a quarter block of ice for our zinc-lined icebox, but they must have drafted his horse for the army. Father now keeps bottles of wine and beer cool with the old army method of wrapping the bottles with wet socks. For some reason, the dripping water keeps it cold.

We still have electricity and cooking gas produced by coal conversion. We have not had any trouble with gas. The Americans have not hit the towering Gasometer at Brigittenau yet. The electricity goes off quite a bit because of the bombing, and I cannot help but think about the poor people in Berlin suffering daily attacks, night and day. We have air-raid alarms once or twice a week now, but the bombers mainly target the industrial areas. If they cannot find or reach their targets, they randomly drop their bombs elsewhere.

Going to school is more of an effort now because of the air-raids, not having streetcars anymore, and all the bombed-out buildings. In one of the school's corridors, I run into Dr. Peter. She is no longer teaching me.

"Hello, Fredi. How is it going?"

Dr. Peter lives in the Fourteenth District where the bomb damage is close to her home.

"Have you heard anything from the Wittmans?"

"That, Fredi, will not be until well after the war, if at all."

Father's main transport contract is the Naschmarkt, the largest vegetable market in the city. Sometimes he manages to get us extra carrots, cauliflower, or a head of lettuce. Anything is welcome, especially anything edible. Potatoes, and sometimes noodles, from the ration card keep us going, combined with bits of this and that, such as breadcrumbs, poppyseeds, or ground nuts.

During one of the raids, Otto and I decide to sneak up onto the flat roof of the six-story tall building where he lives to watch the show. The first pulk of bombers appears, advancing steadily. Little clouds puff up close to them. It is fascinating to watch the shells explode around the steadily moving bombers. One aircraft is hit. It breaks into flames, falls apart, and plummets. There is a strange singing sound in the air.

Horror! Panic!

A deadly rain of jagged steel shell fragments from our anti-aircraft guns falls from the sky, hitting the roof. We fall over each other trying to escape through the door leading to safety. It was a close call and a very bad idea. A bomb could have dropped on the house. Lesson learned. What goes up must come down. Returning home brings a sigh of relief. It is not hit.

At school, there is another alarm. Since we only have a small shelter in the building, students and teachers have to walk double speed for about two blocks to reach cover in a larger communal shelter.

WHAM, WHAM WHAM
WHAM WHAM, WHAM WHAM, WHAM

Pretty close. And then another eight bombs. *Where did they hit?*

As we emerge from the bunker, dust is in the air. Shell fragments on the pavement. Smoke. Soon a big pall of smoke rolls in from the direction of the Fourteenth District. Class closes early. There will be no electricity again. As we pass the Gürtel, we see large clouds of dust and smoke over the Fifth District. I hope Father is all right. He and his truck could be heading in this direction right now.

As I reach our building, everything seems normal. Entering the apartment, I flip the switch. No light. I turn on the gas on the stovetop; there is gas. I rummage for the kerosine lamp, but it has too little kerosine in it. I look for matches but cannot find any. I find a flashlight and luckily the battery still works. I knock on the door of one of our tenants.

"Frau Maier, may I borrow some matches?"

Her husband does not smoke, but everything is in short supply. The Maiers live across the hall, but right now it is just she and her seventeen year old daughter. Herr Maier is in the army. I do not dislike Frau Maier, but she is an awful snoop. Nothing political, but she loves to peek into other peoples' pots—a häferlgucker in the Viennese dialect.

It might only be her need to find new ways to stretch rations. It was she that told me that stinging nettles cook like spinach. She has also mentioned dandelion salad. But where would I find stinging nettles and dandelions in the city?

Back at our place, I scan the larder—slim pickings—some potatoes and band noodles. The Inzersdorfer Band Noodle Factory must have some deal with the government. Thank God noodles are not rationed. I make a roux by putting some flour and water in a jar and shaking it very well. I pull the boiling pot off the fire, let it cool down a bit, and stir the flour-water in. To save nutrients, I no longer peel potatoes. I just scrub them. Potatoes and noodles. Dinner solved.

At dinner, Father tells me about the confusing situation at the market. Losses due to bombing. Railway difficulties. And then he chuckles.

"Something funny happened at the zoo. At one of the last air-raids, they bombed the Schönbrunn Zoo. Among the several hundred squirrels that were killed, there was also an elephant. Now, one of the pub owners at the end of Schönbrunner Street got the clever idea to purchase the meat of the elephant from the zoo administrator. While everything that creeps, flies, oinks or moos is registered on the supplementary section of the ration card, nowhere does it say anything about elephants!

"So the pub owner re-sold most of the meat—there must have been a lot—to his friends and prepared a huge vat of elephant gulyas (goulash). Where he got the onions, the garlic, and the paprika is beyond me. He must have gotten it on the black market—even the amount of salt needed would be a problem. They say that the meat had to be cooked a very long time, and even then it was tough and stringy. Anyway, he got a lot of priceless publicity. He is contemplating changing the name of his inn to 'Zum Elefanten.'"

"Father, would you eat elephant meat?"

"If I was hungry enough, I would eat boiled shoe leather. That beast, the elephant, was probably as tough."

A day later, Father comes home with a pair of wieners which he had traded for some extra heads of lettuce. He is very clever that way, constantly finding new ways to supplement our diet. I find a way to cook everything he scavenges. I wish he would dig up some sauerkraut. I do not like it by itself, but there are many ways to cook with it. He also supplies my aunt with extra food and, as things get tougher, they grow closer again. But I will have to deal with Frau Maier from across the hall. Any waft of non-ration food sparks her interest.

At school, everything is in flux. Two students, Josef Wettl and Pépi Blch, and Dr. Januszek got bombed out of their homes and were, of course, absent. I do not know where any of them live, I think in the Fourteenth District. Since very few people have private telephones, which rarely function anyway, communication is difficult. We own a radio, but the music on it is frequently interrupted by early warning broadcasts and news from the front, which is getting progressively worse and worse.

We have a new teacher, Hannelore Steiner, who will teach us German standard shorthand. We are in the third session with her. She is a good teacher. She hails from a place outside Berlin, from the Altreich, the old Germany, as opposed to the Ostmark (former Austria).

In Vienna, the Bavarians, southern Germans, and even some Rhinelanders are acceptable, but Prussians elicit a vague feeling of animosity in us, an undercurrent against being ruled. A remnant from the days when Maria Theresa fought Frederick the Great for supremacy.

There is a tiny cluster of boys in our class that oppose all Piefkes (slur for Prussians). The rest of us shrug it off, but one day, sitting in Frau Steiner's class, I notice a strong stink coming from the direction of the podium. Frau Steiner gathers her things and calmly walks to the very back of the classroom, still teaching but without the use of the blackboard. The stink gets stronger and stronger. Two boys in the front row cough and choke. No reaction from Frau Steiner. She coughs a bit but carries on.

What is happening?

Finally, the bell rings. I see Frau Steiner walk out the door and hear her coughing in the corridor. Everyone is coughing, choking, and stumbling out. Some boys open the windows. For about ten minutes nothing happens; we go back in. It still stinks, but then all hell breaks loose. The school director, an ultra-National Socialist, red-faced and very agitated, storms into the classroom.

"You communists! You plutocrats!"

New German swear words?

Halfway into his outburst, the air raid sirens come on.

"Order, order!" the director shouts, his head still lobster-red with fury.

We all make it to the shelter, saved from the bombs and the director.

"Hans, what was that crazy stink? It was awful. I thought I was going to choke to death. I certainly admire how Frau Steiner kept her cool."

"Well, Franz Novak—you know, the chemistry nut whose father fell early in the war—devised a fiendish plot against Frau Steiner. He constructed a device that poured sulphuric acid onto some iron filings, rigged to be activated by the desk drawer."

I feel like apologizing to Frau Steiner, but it is hard to meet her alone. The steady tone of the all-clear signal wails. Back to school we go.

After a block, we hear, "Heavens! Look, the school is on fire! Look at that smoke billowing out of the roof!"

As we walk closer, we are stopped by a policeman. We are a large group of boys, ranging in age from eleven to seventeen, a mix of all grades, standing around. A fire engine arrives, teachers carry files and boxes out of the building. The neighbouring house seems to be struck as well, smoke emanating from its roof.

"Go home. Come back on Thursday for classes."

"A cluster of stick bombs hit. Most did not go off. We have the fires under control."

That takes care of the stink incident investigation, for now anyway.

A month ago, everyone got lessons on how to deactivate stick firebombs. The bombs are composed of a thirty centimetre long octagonal stick of magnesium with a heavy iron trigger at the end. Coming down trigger first, the weight of the heavy trigger pierces the roof and maybe one more story. The impact ignites the magnesium which, once burning, reaches temperatures up to a thousand degrees Celsius. Between impact and when it reaches full heat, it is possible to grasp the device and throw it somewhere that it will do less harm. You can also douse the bomb with water if you catch it right after impact. Every house received a bucket and a water pump to keep in their attic.

Luckily, we have not had many canister bombs dropped on Vienna. The canister bombs are the really dangerous ones. That is how those awful fires in Hamburg were able to incinerate whole blocks. We are lucky so far. Our damage is mainly in the outlying districts of Floridsdorf and Simmering. Incendiary bombs are a specialty of the Brits, who bomb at night. We are too far for them.

Father brings home two fish—a trout and a pike.

"Where did you get those?"

"They are bomb victims."

"Bomb victims?"

"Exploding bombs kill the fish. The dead fish float to the surface and often drift to the edge of the water. A friend picked a dozen up after yesterday's bombings in Floridsdorf. I gave one to Aunt Ria and you can cook these for tonight."

Aunt Ria shows me how to cut a fish open and scrape out their guts.

"Since you have no fat, salt the fish and poach it over low heat until it is cooked. Save the broth, put a diced potato into it, and you have soup for tomorrow. That night, I dream of Elék, of Magda and her beautiful fish in sour cream paprika sauce with galuska dumplings on the side.

Father gets other freight jobs besides his contract with the vegetable market. He often gets jobs by frequenting his favourite pub. Despite all the shortages, there is still wine and beer. There are other shortages and delivery problems, but the horse-drawn beer wagons with barrels hanging from their laddered sides still come. The pub owners buy wine directly from the producers in the country. Father is going with his pub owner to Neusiedl am See in the Burgenland to select and buy wine for the pub.

"Do you want to come along, Fredi?"

"I would love to."

Father's snub-nosed Italian Fiat truck with its steering wheel on the right side is hard to drive, especially when passing other vehicles. The driver's seat is also separated from the passenger's seat by the engine hood, making it uncomfortable for a third person to ride in the cab.

Wartime driving is extra difficult in the country. The light shining through small slits on the covered headlights only illuminate about two metres. There are no street lights. All the city streets are paved, mostly with cobblestones, but country roads are gravel. Only roads connecting the major cities are paved with asphalt. There are few road signs. In addition, a good part of the traffic is horse-drawn, so you end up with very slow roads. The only speedy form of transport for both the private sector and the military is the railway.

It is early in the morning. I am excited to get out of the city. At the pub owner's place, we roll two large oak barrels onto the truck's platform, tie them down with ropes, and secure them further with curved wooden wedges.

"Good morning, Herr Wotruba!"

"Good morning. Good that your father let you come with us."

"For the first couple of hours, Herr Wotruba is going to sit in the passenger seat. You will sit behind the hood for a while, until I fix you a seat on the platform."

Driving through the southern outskirts of the city, we are surrounded by the impact of war. Collapsed and damaged buildings, a shattered streetcar on its side. Crews frantically digging through the rubble of a collapsed building, trying to reach survivors. The dust of pulverized mortar hangs in the air like a gritty fog.

The road south is already cleared. Further on, a bombed factory swarms with figures and construction equipment—men working to get it back into production. I remember Josef Zeilinger, a boy in my class. His father's plant manufactures Heinkel fighter plane parts. After his factory was badly damaged, he hoped for at least a month's vacation, but after four days, he was back at work again. They had merely robbed another plant of two key machines.

"The more damage there is, the better we learn to cope," he had said.

The further we get out of town, the more the scene returns to peaceful farmland. We pass into the province of Burgenland. In the past, Burgenland belonged to the kingdom of Hungary until a plebiscite (special referendum) ceded it to Austria in the early 1920s. Neusiedl am See is a town on the shores of Lake Neusiedl, a large, shallow lake which forms the greater part of the border between Germany and Hungary. It is so shallow that you can wade across it in some places. Geologically, it is similar to Lake Balaton in Hungary but smaller.

We arrive at the centre of Neusiedl am See. Herr Wotruba gets out of the truck and asks for the location of the wine distribution agent, the contact coordinator for the winegrowers. There is some gesticulation and pointing from the bystanders. Herr Wotruba gets back in the truck.

After some talk with the wine agent, Herr Wotruba hands Father a list.

"What do you think, Hans?"

Father is not an oenologist, but he knows his wine. There are five good choices. A decision is made. We head for the first winegrower.

"Oh, Herr Wotruba, good to see you again."

They enter the vintner's house for more wine talk. We head for the cellar; I am allowed to come. The cellar is large with an arched ceiling. Variously-sized barrels are lined up in two long rows like soldiers.

At a table up front, the tasting begins. The winegrower produces the first wine. Sniffing, swirling, holding the glass up for colour. Tasting, spitting out. Barrel by chosen barrel, it is an age-old ritual.

Because of my age, I am not a party to the tasting, but I do get a lunch of beautiful home-baked rye bread and bacon. Lovely deep-smoked bacon. Bacon like in Elék. I drink apple cider. I watch the loading of the first cask. A long hose pumps the wine directly into a barrel on the truck.

At the next stop, I decide to skip the cellar tour and sneak in a short walk through town. There is no sign of war here. People go about their daily business as usual. We end up with two casks and two demijohns of wine. Time to drive home. Herr Wotruba and Father seem especially happy.

Have they cheated on the spitting out?

Nearing Vienna, we happen across the final stages of yet another air attack. Clouds of dust and smoke billow. On Simmeringer Hauptstrasse, we are stopped by a police and military roadblock. We have to detour. We arrive back at the pub in the dark. Darkness during blackouts is religiously enforced.

Despite shouts of 'Blackout! Blackout!' from the neighbours, there is little real danger. We are too far for the Brits and the Americans do not like to bomb at night. It is, however, hard to work when it is as dark as the inside of a cow. But, with the help of a pump, hose, and assorted guests (drinking buddies), all the precious liquid reaches Herr Wotruba's cellar, which also doubles as his well-provisioned air-raid shelter. This is the basement where the barrels remain. What a lovely way to get bombed.

I missed school, but it was worth it. Wartime provides many excuses, from the bizarre to the tragic.

We return home to a letter from my mother in Aigen-Schlägl. She, my new little sister, and her three sisters, Anna, Margret, and Mitzi, are doing well there. An American bomber pilot parachuted over town and landed in the market square. He was arrested by a gendarme. Greetings from the grandparents. They see little of the war, occasionally bombers pass high above them.

The mail to and from the front, die Feldpost, functions amazingly well. Given the mobility of the fighting and the fluctuation on the front, it is downright miraculous.

The Swiss, although neutral, have a wonderful organization called The Red Cross which is headquartered in Geneva. They inspect the labour, prisoner, and concentration camps that the Reich allows them to inspect.

They have a postcard system, letting families know whether their family members are still alive. Ilse, Frau Teufelhard's daughter, showed me the one they got from her brother. It said that he was an English prisoner and alive, but nothing more. Not much, but it helped stop them from worrying. This service, however, only works with the western enemies, not with the Soviets.

Uncle Herman is back from the war. He still seems like the old Uncle Herman, calm and reflective. As a journeyman boilermaker, he is well-versed in railway yard metalwork, such as welding and cutting. He was serving in the army's pioneer unit (light engineer unit) and specialized in cutting the steel girders of destroyed bridges and removing metal barricades. Before being recruited into the army, he had worked at a locomotive factory. Locomotives are now the principal transport medium in the Reich.

So why was he not declared 'essential' and kept at home?

I have always liked Uncle Herman. He is always easy-going. He, Aunt Mali, and my cousin Frïeda live within walking distance of our house, on the other side of the railway shunting yard in the Fourteenth District. To get to them, you cross an iron footbridge over the yard. I loved standing on this bridge when I was a little boy, clouded in the steam of locomotives passing under me.

The tale he tells is horrific.

"Never in my life will I forget that last day in Stalingrad. Riddled with shrapnel, bleeding through all my bandages, I was lying on a stretcher in the snow, just one in a long row of wounded, hoping to be flown out. The last JU 52 transport plane was loading. The airstrip was going to be taken by the Soviets at any time.

"The pilot yelled, 'No more or I cannot take off.' Medics were shuffling the wounded inside the plane. 'One more!' they replied. I felt myself being lifted, carried, and shoved into the plane. The door shut. I can still hear the cries of those left behind on the snow. 'Take me, I do not want to die.' Being left while wounded meant certain death.

"I heard the two engines roar unnaturally loudly. We must have overrun the end of the runway. The plane bumped. We flew metres above the ground. Some infantry fire hit the plane and then slowly, very slowly, we gained height, but we were not safe yet. The next few hundred kilometres were still in Soviet air space, but we made it.

"The several months I spent in a Kiev hospital were very pleasant. After that, partly due to my injuries, partly because of my specialty training and experience, I was released from the army on the condition that I returned to a job at the locomotive factory. Locomotives and Tiger tanks rank first."

I am doing worse and worse at school, especially in mathematics. It is a pain. I seem to understand the process, but the result is mostly wrong. Embarrassingly, it is the simple arithmetic in it. I am much better at languages. English and Latin come easily, but I have to work for French.

I dread Physical Education class. I was born with a balance defect, so I have a hard time riding a bicycle or skiing. It always ends badly. I try to avoid team sports because I actually want my team to win! Despite all this, I am relatively popular, accepted for what I am. I must have some desirable qualities.

The war is a dreadful distraction. It is not going well. The places mentioned in the official army bulletin are closer and closer to us.

When and how will all this end?

The aerial attacks on the major German cities are many times heavier and deadlier than what is coming down on Vienna. I wonder how anyone can still go to work amid such infernos. But, as long as we live, our needs go on.

We know where most major Russian cities are from the heady, victorious days of the early Russian campaign. We boys were like generals sticking pins to maps. Now it is going the other way, coming closer and closer to The Fatherland.

Fear of communism is Hitler's strongest weapon. We are a nation of small shopkeepers and independent tradesmen. The adults argue amongst themselves.

"Will communism mean the loss of our spiritual values?"

"Will we become nothing more than cogs in the machine of the state?'

Are we not cogs in the National Socialist state already?

Fate is unstoppable; even we boys sense that.

My grandmother is a Catholic and a monarchist.

"Grandma, the boys are writing a hooked sign on the back of their inkwells."

"Fredi, do not do that. That is the sign of the devil!"

Weeks later, there were hundreds of flags with the sign of the devil on Mariahilferstrasse while Hitler passed a jubilant crowd in his Horch limousine. We are going back to work, he assured us. The depression is over, jobs for all.

The family believes that the plebiscite numbers for the Anschluss —for the annexation of occupied Austria into Germany—announced by the Austrian chancellor might have gotten as high as 75%, but Hitler's report of 99% is certainly fudged.

Father brings home an egg. I have not seen one for some time. I consult with Aunt Ria. She has a little jam left. I have some flour and a small jar of powdered milk. I am going to make crepes for Father. He loves them and has not had any for a long time. But just as I get organized, the air-raid sirens start to wail. Bad timing. I cover my ingredients and the precious egg and open the windows, following the latest instructions. This helps prevent them from being blown out. Down into the cellar we go. I sit next to Aunt Ria. Father is somewhere on the road with his truck. We joke about keeping chickens in our empty stables.

What would we feed them?

Tssk, tssk, tssk, tssk, tssk, tssk, tssk

Anti-aircraft guns. They must be above us.

WHAM WHAM WHAM

A glowing poker stabs my brain. Stab, stab, and then a lesser stab. The ceiling of our primitive shelter vibrates as if it is about to cave in on us. Masonry rains down. Two spidery fissures creep up the wall next to where the second bomb struck.

It is going to cave in on us!

One second, two, then—

Bang, crash, clang, bang, bang, blonk

A mix of shattered masonry and building parts from the neighbouring building has been blown high into the air and come crashing back down on us. We are deafened by the blasts. We sit, stupefied, stunned.

Aunt Ria breaks the silence. "Fredi, are you alright?"

I cannot hear her, but I think that is what she is saying. I do not know how long we sit here, coughing from the dust.

"Is anybody hurt?"

Are we buried?

We all survived. It is now time to find out whether we are buried or have become homeless.

"I am going up!"

I drag myself up the stairs to see if we can get out. Something is blocking the cellar door. I push my weight against it to get it open. Instantly, I am wrapped in a wave of thick dust. The visibility is so bad, I can see less than a metre.

The house looms above me. It is still standing. I go back to the cellar door and call down to the others. They slowly come up. The dust settles a bit. I feel my way up the stairs to the apartment. Looking down from the corridor's shattered windows, I can just barely make out that the roof of the stables at the back of the house, next to our shelter, looks mostly caved in. Debris is everywhere, all over the yard. Piles of it.

Struggling up to the apartment, I find the door open. Did I leave it open? The glass in the apartment windows is not broken. Everything is buried in dust. By great miracle, the egg is not broken, but the rest of the ingredients are scattered.

How in hell am I going to clean this mess?

But we are very lucky. Split seconds one way or another and it could have been the morgue for us or, at best, the bombed-out shelter. I sit on a chair. The world is spinning and I feel like retching. Luckily, I have not got much inside me to retch.

I pull myself together and look for Aunt Ria. I find her on top of the cellar stairs, assisted by Frau Meier. She is badly shaken. I help her to her apartment which is fully intact. It was the furthest from bomb number two.

I hear the other tenants inspecting their apartments which also seem to be alright, except for all the mess of course. Only Frau Meier's apartment has any serious damage, some bad cracks in the walls of a bedroom. I hear ambulances, the people of the bomb squad, and the commanders of various rescue teams who have arrived to dig for survivors shouting orders outside. We are still in the middle of a raid and they are already here. I am impressed.

Wondering what has happened to the neighbouring houses, I open our heavy street door and step outside. The street seems to be in a heavy fog, but it is just the dust in the air. I do not last long outside. In less than a minute, a policeman appears.

"Get back into the house! During damage recovery, no one is allowed outside!"

After recognizing me, the policeman informs me that at the corner house, the one next to us, everyone in the shelter was killed. There are dead in the other neighbouring house too, but they have not reached them yet. Some are buried under tons of debris, but there are also survivors. The ambulance over there has just taken two away.

The adjacent house which got hit by bomb number two is a newer, upscale building with high ceilings, proper bathrooms, and so on. It has a three-sided, five metre airshaft looming above our stables. When the bomb came down, it exploded at the bottom of the airshaft, right at the edge of the building proper. The explosion caved in the ceiling of the air-raid shelter below. It also denuded the walls of the air shaft of tons of stucco, throwing it first up high and then dumping it back down. All this, only ten metres from us in our cellar.

Father appears. "God, am I glad you are alive. Are you hurt in any way?"

"No, just shocked."

"Where and how is Aunt Ria?" Father inspects the rest of the house. He calls for me. "I think there is a dud in the left stable." A good part of the roof is hanging down and there is a round hole in the middle of it that suggests a Blindgänger (a dud). "I hear something ticking. If it is a bomb, it will destroy a good part of the house."

I put my ear close to the pile. "Father, I cannot hear anything. You are very upset. It must be your own heartbeat that you hear."

He goes out onto the street and appeals to the rescue crews to come and see if it is a dud, but they are too busy digging for survivors and tell him that they will come later. Now they must dig for people.

"We must convince them that there really is a bomb! It is just there, where the cows stood." When built, we had left the floor of the stable unpaved so that the cow urine would sink into the ground. "The bomb must have dug itself in."

It could also be a time bomb; they tick, too. We cannot wait for the bomb squad. By then, it might be too late. How do you dig up a two hundred fifty kilogram bomb? Simple. Very, very carefully. If the situation were not so serious, a neutral bystander would have thought that we were performing a comedy act.

"Careful. No, slowly. Slowly."

"Lift that slab, higher. Careful."

"I will get the brick out. Push this clump to the side."

"No, no. Not that far…"

For an hour and a half, the two of us play Russian roulette with this pile of bricks and crap. Finally, 'Eureka!' we unearth a perfectly round granite ball, thirty centimetres in diameter. The Americans do not drop granite balls. They are much more advanced than that. It must be a roof decoration. That explains the strange clunk noise I heard after the flying debris came back down.

Two days later, a sergeant from the bomb squad arrives at our house. "I understand you have a dud here. Yes, that is a dud all right."

Father decides that we should clean up the yard. We have a large, empty dung pit at the back of the yard, leftover from the days when we had cows. We remove the heavy boards covering it and start to fill it with dust and debris. Father and I work like slaves filling it. He shovels and I wheel it away, alternating between two wheelbarrows. Our back yard is paved with cobblestones and it is hard to pick up the dust between them.

That night I find it hard to get to sleep, but when I finally do, a ghastly nightmare haunts me. I see a group of uniformed men sorting out a pile of debris. One holds up a dismembered foot. "By the size of it, it must be Fredi."

The rescue service removes some of the restrictions, so Father goes to see Herr Kübel. He doesn't say much when he gets back home. Father is very distraught about the Lichtneggers. Karl is in the army. The third one in this friendship trio, Herr Kübel, owns a hat-making shop. He lives just a couple of blocks up on Aegidigasse. I used to visit him often, but all of a sudden, I was not allowed to visit him anymore. He is half Jewish and very afraid of being deported. He avoids attention, but people still buy his hats. You have to have a black hat when you go to a funeral, and these days there are a lot of funerals.

"Terrible, horrible."

Father is distraught. The rescue people are still sorting body parts and trying to identify individuals. We may only pass on the opposite side of the street and are not allowed to linger.

The third day after these latest bombs, I walk past the house where the first bomb struck. Many of the inhabitants were away from home when the bomb hit and are in shock to find family members macerated to a pulp and blended into the rubble.

Some are trying to salvage whatever goods they can. Most of the building's front is sheared off, exposing the inside of apartments and making the building look like a giant dollhouse. On the second floor, three men are trying to secure a grand piano that is hanging half over the edge of the sheared floor. It is Frau Kienberger's piano, the piano teacher. She was a very nice old lady. I hope she is now teaching the angels Chopin's etudes. Miraculously, in the back of some apartments, pictures still hang on the walls, the glass intact. A modern radio lies crushed by fallen furniture. I wonder how long the owner had to save for it.

The greatest tally for the neighbourhood's tragedy is at the corner house where eighteen people were fragmented. No survivors. Among the dead are the parents of Karl Lichtnegger, my father's best friend.

In the other adjacent house, eight are dead, crushed by a cement ceiling that caved in on them. Six people are injured, two seriously. Bernhard's printshop on the ground floor is partly destroyed.

One house further down has no casualties, but the workshops in the back are destroyed. Two more bombs were dropped in this series —the third on a pastry shop at Wallgasse and the final one on a house on the Gürtel, next to where my aunt Poldi lives.

I am deeply sad that the Bernhard foreman is one of the victims and devastated about the ghastly demise of the Lichtneggers. They were always very kind to me when I was a small child and they werea large part of the landscape of my childhood. Now they cannot even have a funeral.

I spend another day in the house, cleaning up. Father has engaged one of his pub friends to assist us. We have plenty of tools left from the dairy days. Wheelbarrows, picks, pitchforks, shovels, and brooms make the job easier. I am still quite jittery and distracted. I do not sleep well. I could sorely use a bath and a week at Aigen-Schlägl with my mother, a place where there is no war. I wish Mother were here to look after the food and the apartment. It would make things much easier for me.

How am I going to put up with school after all this?

There is too much bloody stress and distraction. The tedium of school contrasts with the heavy emotions of the day. It is easy to skip school. The excuse now is the almost daily air-raid sirens. A day of rest is not easy. Little can calm you when the days passing by are punctuated with yet another trip to the cellar, another set of flak fire, and the sound of impacting bombs. Most of the time they are bombing somewhere else, but the mere presence of enemy aircraft triggers the alarm. I often arrive at school an hour late. Nowadays the teachers accept any excuse. They are in the same leaky boat.

Since alarms have become a daily distraction, some are at school, some are not. For a student already in trouble, especially in mathematics and the sciences, every missed lesson makes it beastly hard to catch up. We have some brainiacs in class that seem to manage, but I suspect there is some parental tutoring involved there.

I do not have that luxury. Even Aunt Ria, who has more schooling than Father, does not remember much mathematics and physics anymore. History, languages, and the arts are not much of a problem for me, but the sciences are. We have thirteen subjects.

Each one, if failed, can block a student from advancing to the next grade.

Everything is stressful. I want more time just hanging out with the boys. The Hitler Youth training is a pain in the butt. I do not like playing soldier.

Tonight I listen to the army bulletin about heavy bombing, day and night, in some of the northern cities and think about how well off we are comparatively. The Brits have not gotten to us yet. We can still sleep at night.

ALPINE BOOT CAMP AND DITCH-DIGGING

4

THE WAR GOES on, badly. The air raids become more and more frequent. They have not carpet-bombed us yet. Father is very busy these days with the market and a wide assortment of other freight. He has a part-time swamper now to assist him with the heavy lifting. Seldom can he sneak in an hour at the pub.

I sort of manage between school, homework, the house, and the sundry annoyances of wartime daily life. I am annoyed that I cannot just hang out with my friends, play games, or do anything not connected with war. Coming home from school, I find a letter addressed to me. Its message is simple: 'Report to the recruitment centre, address and date below.'

From the information given to us, I will be taken to a Wehrertüchtigūngslager (pre-military boot camp) at the Planneralm in Styria above Judenburg for a two week training camp.

Damn, that is all I need.

The next day at school, I ask Otto whether he has received a similar notice. Neither he nor any of my close friends were called. This is the army; they got me at random from a mailing list. There is a list of what I need to bring. The cheap buggers do not even supply uniforms and boots. They even have the gall to demand food ration stamps for the whole period.

The worst part is that I will not have any of my friends with me for support. It is always easier if the guy suffering next to you is a longtime pal that you can trust. It could be worse. Thankfully, I am too young for the Reich Arbeitsdienst (Labour Service) and it is the army, not the SS. Father drives me to the recruitment centre.

"Be careful. Try not to stand out in any way. Do not volunteer for anything."

After getting a hug from Father, I enter the building.

A soldier at the vestibule asks, "Training camp? The hall one flight up, to your left."

The hall is crowded with boys and military personnel—a master sergeant in charge and about ten lance corporals. All of them seem to be wounded soldiers from the front, re-classified to home defence. There are between fifty and sixty boys.

The sergeant calls out, “Boys, make formation.”

Instant confusion. We do not know each other and push each other into a rough line. Unfortunately, because of my height, I become the head of the line which I deplore.

Are there no other tall boys?

“Heil Hitler. You have been chosen for pre-military training as a first step toward making you ready for the defence of The Fatherland. You will taken by train to Judenburg in Styria. From there, you will be take a bus to the Planneralm camp.”

Two buses take us to the Southern Railway Station. We board our train. Crammed into compartments, we have a chance to get acquainted and to discuss the situation My new comrades are all Viennese, but from different districts. We will not get paid because we are not part of the army yet.

A guy called Tony tells us about his cousin Siegfried’s experience when he was at the camp we are heading for. “It was dehumanizing and exhausting to the point where you want to strangle the torturer.”

This prospect makes it hard to digest the sandwiches we get. I wonder how they selected us. In my case, it is certainly not for leadership qualities. The boys I manage to talk to have very different backgrounds. None of them have an outstanding record in the Hitler Youth. Reinhard Eppinger lives in the Thirteenth District and goes to a classical high school—Latin and Greek with only one other foreign language. Josef Hawatil is a second-year mason’s apprentice. Richard Unger is studying to be an electrician. And so on.

None of them seemed to be particularly athletic; none made their class soccer team. There must be some method to the selection madness. None of the boys have been on KLV, as I was in Hungary. Nearly all the boys’ fathers are in the army, several killed in action. Two of the boys are bombed out and live with relatives.

Leopold Elch is from Meidling and knows my schoolmate, Pepi Resch, whose father owns the Café Resch in Meidling. He tells me that Otto Skorzeny, the war hero who freed Mussolini, dropped in for a visit. The table where he sat all the years he was an architect, his Stammtisch (reserved table), now has a plaque with his name on it.

We are being shepherded by a corporal and a private. They are responsible for keeping us together, fed, and out of trouble. As we approach Wiener Neustadt—

WHAM WHAM WHAM WHAM WHAM
TAK TAK TAK TAK TAK TAK TAK

"They are bombing the Messerschmitt factory!"

We are a few kilometres away from the target, but nevertheless, the train comes to a halt. We can hear and see the planes flying overhead. B-17s fly in pulk formation high above. Artillery shells explode around them. P-51 Mustang fighters swarm, protecting them. But this fascinating spectacle is abruptly disturbed.

"Are you crazy? Get down as low as you can! Cover your head with your arms." The loud and stern voices of our keepers bring us back to reality. "You might not be the target, but in an air attack, you never know what will come down where. Some fighter pilot might want to bag another locomotive. They are even more expensive than tanks."

As soon as the war around us subsides and we start to relax, another wave appears. The intensity and accuracy of our anti-aircraft artillery are formidable. Finally, the attack is over. We are rolling again. A crashed bomber two hundred metres from us is still burning. There is a lot of smoke.

We pass through the peaceful countryside again. In the distance, we can see Schneeberg, the highest mountain in Lower Austria. I remember a lovely school excursion there when I was in elementary school, a long weekend with parents and teachers at Rax, the mountain next to the Schneeberg.

We change trains at Bruck an der Mur. From there we proceed to Judenburg. As we arrive, it is dark. Very dark. The blackout is everywhere, even in Judenburg. We wait at the station. After a while, buses arrive to take us to the camp. Our keepers, still with us, take roll call. It is easy to get lost in the darkness of war. We climb into the busses. With the blackout, we can only guess where we are.

After the little hamlet of Irdning, the road gets narrower and narrower, steeper and steeper, as we climb up a mountain. Finally, we are at the Planneralm. The contours of buildings. Beneath our feet, a paved square. I have a creepy feeling that we shall remember this place long after we survive it.

We are led into a spacious room, the mess hall. We line up for our first meal, ladled and handed out on metal plates. Two women and a male cook are in charge of the food. According to my father, the Planneralm—the highest mountain resort in Austria—served as a training camp for the 1936 Austrian Olympic team.

"Hard to breathe, isn't it?"

At two thousand metres above sea level, the air is much thinner here. Our supper is beef soup with noodles and two slices of rye bread. The sergeant who brought us here separates us into three huts.

"Alfred Penz, hut two, bed six."

We are shown our cots and narrow lockers. It looks like a nineteenth century hospital ward. We receive two rough army blankets, a towel, a sheet, a cake of standard-issue soap—the one that does not foam—and a strange, long nightshirt. It has been a long day, though, so we are ready to sleep on anything. I wake, shivering, at three in the morning. I feel like I am sleeping on a block of ice.

BRRRRRRR!!!!!!!!!

The loudest bell I have ever heard wakes us.

"Out of bed! Out of bed! At attention in front of your bed!"

The sergeant pulls our blankets off.

"I will begin by teaching you to fold blankets according to regulation."

He folds two blankets and walks by us, demonstrating the neatness of the exact folds.

"The blanket and the sheet must be folded like this and must be positioned fifteen centimetres from the side and end of the bed. Now get dressed and proceed to the mess hall in precisely eleven minutes. When you hear the bell again, proceed to the square and stand in formation."

Breakfast is two slices of bread, a little dollop of sugarless jam, and a tin cup of ersatz coffee. Minutes later, we are standing in formation. Being the tallest, I am at the front edge, a lightning rod for military fury. Out he comes, the man who is our commander.

"Good morning, men!"

"Good morning, Herr Staffmastersergeant."

"My name is Staffmastersergeant Heinrich Hofbauer, and my job is to turn you sad lot into men who are not killed on the first day you are sent to the front. You will learn to follow orders, regardless of how silly they seem to you. If I order you to stick your head in a toilet you will stick your head in a toilet. Sergeant Moltinger and Sergeant Mayer will command most of the details. Is that understood?"

"Jawohl, Herr Staffmastersergeant."

He does not look very martial. He walks with a distinct limp and seems to have trouble with his left arm, but he wears the Iron Cross, First and Second Class, and the Bronze Close Combat Badge. That means that he has survived hand-to-hand combat more than ten times. Both of the sergeants are wounded soldiers from the front. They have the Iron Cross, First Class. Sergeant Moltinger has lost his left arm from the elbow down.

It is time for the circus to begin. We stand in formation.

"Stillgestanden!" (Attention!)

"Rechts um!" (Turn right!)

"Im Laufschritt marsch!" (Forward at a slow run!)

He jogs with us to the end of the square and from the square to the bottom of a hill.

"See the path up this slope? Run up the path as fast as you can until you reach a rock with a cross painted on it. There, turn around and make it back down as fast as you can. Be careful, it is slippery. Do not break your neck. That is not in the manual. Once you have reached the bottom, turn around and run up the slope a second time. I shall be waiting for you here at the bottom."

It is quite a steep grade. After ten metres uphill, we all feel the altitude. Some break into a fast walk. Everyone is panting.

"This must be the rock!"

We have covered at least five hundred metres. Surprisingly, I am not the worst one in the group. I am used to doing long walks in the mountains and have strong legs. On the way down, on my second round, I meet boys still on their initial way up.

Can you have a heart attack at our age?

Slowly everybody makes it down—except a guy from hut three who slid going downhill, hit his head, and sprained his left ankle.

Maybe that's the way to get through all this.

A whistle. Assembly.

"Spread out for push-ups. Twenty push-ups, everyone."

I try. I just do not have the power. The boys on my left and right are pumping away. Tony is up to twelve. I manage one and a half, which brings more insults from the sergeant.

"What is wrong with you slackers? Have you city boys never done a day's strenuous work? We will toughen you up soon enough."

Time for dinner—pea soup without ham and bread. Maybe they think we are hams enough. Finally, it is bedtime. Maybe I will dream of something far away from this place, but these hard cots are nightmare factories.

BRRRRRRRRRRR

That nasty clock again.

Are they crazy? Will it be every day at three in the morning?

"Everyone outside!"

Freezing in the icy mountain air, clad only in our flimsy nightshirts, we are at the whims of a sadist. Down, up, down, up. We scramble up and down off the hard ground.

Roll forward. *Man, this is downright indecent.* Roll backwards. *This should be forbidden.*

I never could do somersaults, not even when fully dressed. I get stuck in my nightshirt with my arse high up in the air and my long legs wiggling in a frenzy, trying to complete the roll, exposing all that is dear to the public. While this is going on, the others are back to the rise and drop maneuver again.

"My willie is frozen hard. It is going to drop off."

That is one way to get a hard-on.

Our nightshirts are dirty and wet. We are miserable and very cold. I think I might need a blowtorch to ever get warm again.

"Back to the barracks. You have ten minutes to get dressed."

In ten minutes, we are standing at attention in front of our beds, facing the scolding snarl of one of the sergeants.

"Your beds are not made at all, let alone the proper distance from the edges. Get undressed. Fold your clothes. Make your beds. I will see you outside, in your nightshirts, in ten minutes."

Dress. Make your beds. Make your beds again. And again. Make your beds again.

Another day, another form of torture. Today's special is getting flat on the ground and creeping forward, propelling yourself by elbows and knees while crouched as close to the ground as possible, holding a stick that simulates a rifle.

After three-quarters of an hour, the sergeants snarls, "You are lucky. In the regular army, they fire machine guns thirty centimetres over you to keep your heads down."

At the command, 'Sprungauf. Marsch. Marsch!' we scramble up and run like banshees. Crash on the ground. Grapple ourselves up, repeating the same exercise over and over from one the end of the parade ground to the other and back again. After an intermittent short run for diversion, we return to the same misery. Back and forth, back and forth.

"Wegtreten!" (Dismissed)

No one is interested in our lunch of pea soup.

As far as military imagination goes, I must say that there is a lot of variety. They certainly make sure we do not get bored. This afternoon, we are introduced to the wall. I had wondered why there is a wooden wall fifteen metres wide and one and a half metres high at the end of the parade ground. It is too short to be a fence. Little did we know that we would soon call it the 'wall of woe.'

Our assignment is to scale the wall, run the perimeter of the parade ground, scale the wall, and run again. Climb, run, climb, run in a round-robin fashion while another group does the knees-elbows crawling exercise in the parade ground's centre.

How the hell am going to tackle that dumb wall?

It is not easy going and I am 1.82m tall. Our smallest boy, Franz Novak, is maybe 1.50m. He is also the youngest, born on Christmas Day, 1929. He looks barely twelve and dislikes being here more than any of us.

I quickly think the problem over. If I try from a standing position, I will not have the power in my arms to pull and push myself high enough to get over the top. The only way I can possibly make it is with the run, jump, and turn method. If I hurt myself, maybe all the better. I just do not want to break my neck.

I jump higher than I have ever jumped before, grab the top rail of the wall, rise and turn using my momentum, and swing my right leg over. I am now almost on top with part of one leg over and one leg behind. I try to slide myself over to the other side, but even with both of my hands clinging to the top, and my right leg hooked on top, I have no leverage. I try pulling myself up but fail. Desperate, I let go, hoping that I can twist my body and land on at least one foot. It works. Stumbling forward, I break my fall by pushing my hands against the ground. In two seconds, I am up and running around the parade ground for the next go-around at the over the wall neck-breaker.

Some of the boys do very well. One or two may have had some previous training from escaping over a wall after stealing apples. Others make it after one or two tries. Only one boy did not make it at all. All of us are hurting, though. Black and blue spots are our medals from the wall. As to Novak, one of his friends gave him a leg up. When it comes to Novak, the sergeants turn a blind eye.

Today we get a physical break. It is firearms instruction and training day. This is a very welcome change because it does not require any strenuous movements. We begin with a lecture about the overall organization of the army and the Waffen-SS. We learn about the command structure of military units, the ranks and insignias, and about infantry strategies from battalions to squads. I find it interesting that only a quarter of the Armed Forces are at the fronts. The rest is in garrison units—support, Air Force, flak, logistics, medical, quartermaster, and so on.

In weapons training, we work in groups, because there are not enough weapons at the camp. Our group's first subject is an introduction to the Karabiner 1889 infantry rifle, called the 89k. Taking apart, cleaning, and reassembling rifles is tedious, but it is better than the physically torturous and punishing exercises.

"We do not have enough rifles for everyone, so different groups will work with different weapons. You will be able to disassemble and clean the 89k in your sleep, and at the end of this exercise, we will have a contest. The fastest boy to have the rifle re-assembled gets a knackwurst with mustard."

I was not the worst at this task, but I did not get the sausage. Two other boys did. The sergeant's stopwatch clocked the two exactly the same. Since there was only one sausage, the boys had to share it—the mustard, too.

It is our turn now to get instruction on the MG 34, the MG 42, and the new Sturmgewehr 44 assault rifles.

"We will now show you how to change barrels. You will not get a chance to fire these weapons, but you will see them fired. The MG 42 fires one thousand rounds a minute. You will be familiarized with the enemy's basic weapons and how to attack them. You will learn to tell a T-34 from a T-72 tank and how to destroy them."

"And last, you will see the latest Panzerfaust 60 anti-tank gun fired. You will learn how they are assembled, disassembled, activated, and fired. Unfortunately, we do not have enough, so you do not get to fire them. Tanks are usually accompanied by infantry, either sitting on or following them. If your attack is from a foxhole, you must remember that you will need time to aim the weapon. The Panzerfaust will penetrate most western tanks from any side. The latest T-34s and T-72s are vulnerable from the sides, the back and sometimes the tracks. We have had great success with this weapon."

A lecture familiarizes us with the enemy's most common weapons. We are shown an American Tommy gun, pictures of a Kalashnikov attack rifle, and the standards of the American Army, the M1 and M16 automatic rifles.

I cannot help but think, '*Do they want me, a boy, to fight soldiers armed with all that modern hardware? Are they really going to arm me with a heavy, cumbersome, bolt action Mauser 89k that was already out of date years before the First World War and only slightly modified in 1934?'*

A Panzerfaust lies on the table. Sergeant Moltinger picks it up, twists the head to the left, and the weapon comes apart, exposing its fins and a hollow containing two capsules—one large and one small.

"See the hole on the end of each capsule? When the two holes face each other, the weapon is armed. All you need to do is twist the head back in by turning it to the right. Then you are ready to fire."

So far I have not been good at anything, and sometimes ridiculously bad, but I am accepted and helped by my fellow inmates. But when we head for the shooting range, I feel confident. I know what I can do with my own .22 rifle. The 89k is just a larger calibre.

We line up at the range. When my turn comes, I get into a prone position, check my sights and fire, repeat and fire, repeat and fire until I empty the magazine. The sergeant and corporal examine the target. The centre of the target block is now just one large hole.

"This is somewhat unusual. Can you repeat that for us?"

I calmly and carefully repeat the procedure. This time, four shots are again in the centre and the fifth is at the inside of the black circle.

"In all my time here, I have never seen shooting like this. You will certainly qualify for sharpshooter."

For me, it was not that big of a deal. I am blessed with 20/20 vision.

That evening, the commandant passes me and says, “Nice shooting, Penz.”

I feel satisfaction at finally being allowed to do something where I am not one of the last in the group. I try not to take the praise too seriously. We are still civilians, after all, and not part of the army.

We are all dead tired.

The very next day the weather turns—strong gusts, icy winds. We are two thousand metres up in the Styrian Alps without the right clothes or boots, just our Hitler Youth winter uniforms. It would upset my mother to see me crawling around on the ground. I hope that we are not forced outside. I think the people in charge really do not care about individuals. I shudder to think about our army, outside in the mud, snow and ice, clad only in their summer uniforms, during their first Russian winter.

Thank heavens! It looks that they are not chasing us outside today. But then again, you do not have to be outside in terrible weather to be angry and miserable.

“Bed inspection!”

For bed inspection, Sergeant Moltinger rules with his ruler. My blanket is limp and two centimetres too far from the edge of the bed. We make the beds; he messes them up. He believes in collective guilt. If one boy messes up, we all pay. Four times in a row. We are as angry as the gusts outside. I glance at Franz next to me. He looks like he is going to hit the sergeant. But orders must be followed, no matter how stupid.

The next day, the weather improves and we are exposed to the elements again, repeating the same exercises again and again. However miserable, degrading, trying, and insulting this life is, it becomes routine. The mind adjusts. And everything comes to an end, including our alpine misery. It is good to be going home. Finally, the day has come. I hope I still have a home. We assemble, standing at attention.

Staffmastersergeant Hofbauer gives his farewell address.

“If there is anyone among you who does not hate me, I have done a bad job. This was to prepare you for more of the same when you get called to serve in the regular army. Superior training, discipline, and dedication are the basics of an efficient army. That is why the Prussian Army was a better fighting force.

"You must hunt like a pack of wolves, wired by instinct to each other's moves. This is why orders must be obeyed without question. You must become a cog in a well-oiled fighting machine. War is not for the timid. They are the ones who get themselves killed first.

"Look at the paratroopers at Monte Cassino. A less prepared unit would have been overwhelmed in days. I wish you all the best and hope that all of you survive the war."

I am glad to go home. I understand now that it was all a character-building exercise.

Was it useful?

It will be useful, if the war lasts long enough for me to be called up, and it might help me to better understand the daily Wehrmachts-bericht (Armed Forces Report).

Days go by and the air-raids become more frequent. More and more people from school and family friends have been bombed out and are now sleeping with relatives. Since most Viennese apartments are very small, having extra people means they must sleep on the floor. It is stressful for everyone.

I am getting further and further behind with my school work, but I am not the only one. Subjects like mathematics suffer the most from gaps and absence from lectures. Travelling to and from school is at times an obstacle course.

Father has been sick several times. We both drink a foul-tasting herbal tea now to help with gastric problems. We miss Mother very much, but with a new baby, she is better off where she is. She sends the odd letter.

Aunt Ria is the nurse in the family. She is not a trained nurse, but she has taken care of her ailing mother for several years and looked after Grandfather who suffered from dementia. So far we have not lost any family members.

Father is thinking of getting a second truck and hiring a driver, but this is difficult. The news from the front is not good. The Russians are fighting our army in Budapest. We hear they are destroying that beautiful city. It is only a question of time, a short time, before they appear at our gate. Apprehension rises like steam in a kettle.

“Father, should we pack up and move west? Maybe to Aigen-Schlägl where we can join Mother?”

“No, I think we are better off in a large city.

DITCH DIGGING

And then it comes again, the call from the Hitler Youth Centre: "You are recruited for Schanzen (building defences)."

Some of the party's higher-ups have had the crazy idea to recruit us, the Hitler Youth, to dig anti-tank ditches. Strategically, the enemy will advance through the large, hundred kilometre wide gap between Lake Neusiedl in the south and the Danube River in the north. Even if it were somehow possible to fortify that whole distance, I do not see how all the boys in Vienna could dig an effective defensive system. The distance from Neusiedl am See to Kittsee is twenty kilometres, at least, as the crow flies. To us, it is just another annoyance that will put us even further behind in school. I simply cannot believe it.

I phone Otto to confirm. "Otto, did you receive an order for Schanzen?"

"Yes."

I talk to Father about the situation.

"You cannot get out of it unless you have Dr. Dirschmied (our family doctor) give you a valid medical reason. If the other boys are going, there will not be any classes anyway. If I were you, I would go since then you will be with your friends."

"This time I will not wear my boots. What should I wear that would make them give me a new pair of boots or even a decent used pair?"

"I think there is a pair of Grandfather's patent leather shoes around here somewhere."

So I report for defence of The Fatherland with my feet clad in a pair of my grandfather's old patent leather shoes. One by one, we appear at the Hitler Youth Centre.

"Hahahaha. Look! My God. Fredi Penz is wearing a pair of patent leather shoes!"

"Have you seen Penz in his patent leather shoes?"

"Are you crazy, Fredi? Those shoes are going to come apart as soon as it rains."

The leader of our group asks, "What are you up to? Are you trying to dodge the service?"

"No, Gefolgschaftsführer. My only boots have a large hole in them and the sole has come loose. I have no alternative, but I wanted to come."

So without anticipating it, I become a celebrity. Everyone, everywhere, wants to see the guy with the Lackaraber (Viennese for patent leather shoes). After a while, you can get used to everything, even to being a curiosity—such as the bearded lady at the freak show at the Prater Amusement Park.

"Have you seen the guy in the patent leather shoes?"

We hear that we will go to Neusiedl am See on the very northern end of the lake. We load into buses and head off to build the Reich's defences. The landscape is bucolic. All is peaceful—except for the usual reminders, such as a burned-out Liberator bomber and bombed-out buildings—and uneventful.

Alois Kraizer sings part of a popular ditty, Eine Entdeckungsfahrt ins Grüne, which means something like 'an adventure trip into the green.' This inspires Walter Berry to give us a short rendition of an opera piece that he frequently practices. He is a very promising basso.

We reach Neusiedl am See where Father and I once fetched wine with the pub owner. It is the market town for the region, known for its Grüner Veltliner grapes and annual tulip festival, now put on hold for the duration of the war.

In Neusiedl am See, we stop in front of Party Headquarters. Divided into groups, we are told that we will be billeted in local barns. Our group leader is only eighteen or nineteen. He is very much one of us. We are given blankets and are taken to a large farm and winery. The farmer, Herr Poldinger, greets the assembled two squads.

"As you see, we have spread a comfortable layer of straw for you. With a blanket on top, it should be quite comfortable. There is a stack of sacks near the barn door. Fill a bag with enough hay to form a pillow. When you leave, empty, fold, and return the bags to where you found them. Given your age, I need not tell you that there will be absolutely no smoking in or around the barn. The toilets are between the barn and the winery."

A truck arrives with picks and shovels. A digging we shall go. We march off to invade the countryside. Everywhere I go, I arouse hilarity with my patent leather shoes. The pointing fingers and giggling are embarrassing. I feel like Bozo the Clown in the Sarrasani circus. But it was my own stupid idea.

Arriving at our destination, we find a two hundred metre long area staked out with wooden poles. Strategically placed northeast of the town, the area faces the direction from which the enemy is expected, but also in such a way so as to not unroot any of the precious vines. The local party leader might sport the golden party badge, but he is also a farmer among farmers, and farmers are known for their bauern-schlauheit (shrewdness). An order is an order and it must be obeyed, even by party leaders.

How are they going to deal with several hundred city boys that have never held a shovel or pick in their hands?

There is no Arbeitsdienst at age seventeen anymore—those mandatory months in every German boy's life once spent doing physical labour like digging ditches. Boys now go straight to war.

Everyone gets either a shovel or a pick. The ditch is to be V-shaped, two metres deep at the centre and four metres wide. The excavated earth is heaped on either side of the ditch so that it can be filled back in after the war. We work in teams of two, a pick guy and a shovel guy. The pick guy loosens the earth and the shovel guy scoops it out. It does not work well. Some teams catch the rhythm a bit, most do not.

At lunchtime, some women from the defence committee bring us sandwiches. Good, home-baked bread with butter and apricot jam and an apple. They also bring buckets of drinking water with communal cups attached.

In the afternoon, some of the townspeople arrive to show our leaders how to dig and move earth. They, in turn, will instruct us. At the end of this first day, we walk back to the farm in formation, but not really in step.

Supper cooked by the local women's committee awaits us—slices of lovely home-baked bread and homemade soup with a lot of meat in it. We fall asleep easily. The straw is soft enough, but later in the night—

Hachoo hachoo hachoo

"What is going on?"

"I think it is Ottinger. I believe he has hay fever."

"Erich, hold your nose. Maybe it will go away."

"Can we isolate him somehow?"

"I think it is the hay in the pillow. Erich forget about that hay pillow. Roll up your pants and use that as a pillow instead."

That seems to help. We wake to a sunny day. Yesterday's instruction makes quite a difference. We are really moving now, but I wonder how we are going to move the earth up and out once we get deeper. A tractor with a steel blade would do a better job. During our break, Berry breaks into a beautiful Russian ballad. I think it is one from Eugene Onegin.

"Walter, sing something Italian. Otherwise, the locals will think the Russians are already here."

Our muscles ache"I am really stiff and my back hurts."

"I would not mind a day off to loosen up."

The town's party leader appears to check on our progress.

"Good work, keep it up." He spies my patent leather shoes. "Oh, you are the boy with the patent leather shoes. I heard about you."

"I bet you did. I think the whole district has by now."

"I will ask around and see if any of my friends have a pair of old rubber boots. That would be better than what you have on your feet right now. What shoe size are you?"

"Fifty six."

That is the last I see or hear of him.

Walter Berry and I are a team. He uses the pick and I use the shovel. He loosens the earth and I scoop it with my shovel and swing it up over the top. Just as I move to get my shovel under some loosened earth—

I am thrown forward. A terrible pain spreads through my spine and I pass out. When I come to, I am lying on top of the ditch with everyone gathered around me. Walter is hovering above me.

"Fredi, I am so sorry. I hit you in the back with my pick. I am so sorry. I was not looking."

"It is alright Walter. I know you did not mean it."

I cannot move. I vaguely feel someone taking my shoes off, and now I cannot feel anything.

Am I paralyzed?

The thought makes me pass out again.

When I come to, I am on a stretcher in an ambulance on the way to the hospital.

"Where am I going?"

I feel myself being lifted and put on an operating table.

I am in a bed. The clean smell of the sheets calms me. They must have sedated me. I hurt a lot.

"There you are, the boy with the patent leather shoes. I heard about you."

"I bet you have."

"You are going to be alright. Your belt saved you from being paralyzed. There is a square hole through your belt and into your skin." (I will always have the scar.) "It was quite a shock to your nervous system. As for your patent leather shoes, they are there in your locker. You might consider donating them to the Neusiedl am See Museum."

After a few days, my condition improves. Kindness and tender loving care help a lot. I even have visitors. The food is good and the care is remarkable. I have no desire to leave. In about ten days, after some additional treatments, I am nearly fully recovered. I am, however, forbidden from doing any more manual labour during our time in Neusiedl am See.

That is good news and bad. I do not fancy shovelling, but I do not want to appear to be a malingerer. The hospital lends me some crutches. At least I do not have to worry about appearances now.

After saying goodbye and being kissed by my nurses, I get a ride back to the farm. I spend that whole day chatting with the farmer and his wife. He has known the wine-buying pub owner in my neighbourhood for a long time and vaguely remembers my father.

In the evening, the crew returns and cheers to find me here.

"It is so great to see you walking. I felt so guilty after I hit you."

"Do not worry, Walter. You did not mean it, and I am alright."

After three more days, we head back to Vienna. The boys might not have dug an anti-tank trench from Neusiedl am See to Kittsee as the Gauleiter (District Leader) might have wished, but the boys did dig a nice, shorter one—a 'Grosse Gruam' as we say in Viennese—a big ditch.

THE BOY SOLDIERS

5

VIENNA, MARCH 1945
THE ENEMY IS AT THE GATE

THE RUSSIANS HAVE crossed the German border and are already in the Burgenland. News from Eastern Prussia of retribution, torture, mutilation, and rape poisons the public mind. Magnified by further propaganda, nightmares of the invading Asiatic horde instill a will to fight to the death in everyone. Hitler declares Baldur von Schirach, the former Reich Youth Leader and a member of Hitler's inner circle, the new Reich Commissioner for the Defence of Vienna.

The curtain is up for the last act. The so-called Southeast Wall, the series of ditches and earthworks dug and built by thousands of Hitler Youth and foreign labourers, stretches from Neusiedl am See to Kittsee. The regular troops which remain to defend the city are, at best, at half to quarter strength.

Who says there are no more reserves? I wonder.

There are units of Eastern Fascists of all stripes—including the Vlasov, the Arrow Cross, and the Ustaše—and also the very young. The Hitler Youth, children indoctrinated from ten years on to obey any order, are conveniently outfitted in their winter uniforms.

Are they not a fighting force? Call them up. They will fight to the death.

There is also the Volkssturm (People's Storm), volunteer units of older gentlemen who serve in civilian dress and are identified only by their 'Volkssturm' armbands and carry 89k rifles. They personify German schoolbook lore, especially when seen carrying Panzerfausts in propaganda films.

For the war machine, the best part is they can get away with not paying any of them. Hitler Youth and Volkssturm members receive no pay, no Armed Forces uniform, and no military identification. Just get them fired up and throw them to the dogs. It will prolong the lives of the men in charge for days, maybe even weeks, but at best a month.

The leadership is clear of the charge of using soldiers under the legal limit of sixteen because, officially, they are not part of the regular army. They ignore the Geneva Convention that declares combatants not in uniform and without proper papers to be outlaws. If the Russians kill any of them, it is just collateral damage. The Hitler Youth boys and the older Volkssturm gentlemen are at greatest risk whenever they get separated from their units.

There is one factor that the party's leaders and generals underestimate, however, and that is local resistance. A good part of the Viennese army garrison, some of its generals, and even a few local party leaders are not willing to see Vienna destroyed. This is Vienna, their home. Furthermore, a sizable part of the population has become disillusioned lately with Hitler and is motivated to prevent Vienna from becoming another Fortress Breslau. No Fortress Vienna. Despite the zealots, more and more people want Vienna declared an 'Open City'—a city that has announced an end to all defensive efforts, to avoid total destruction in war.

The mood is grim in the Penz household. Father is upset—worried about me, Aunt Ria, and the tenants of the house. Father's favourite pub is still open and is now an underground information hub, keeping a pulse on current events. I doubt he is telling me everything. The city has a million eyes and ears; they are everywhere and nowhere.

"Fredi, you might not like what I am about to tell you, but I have to. I do not feel safe anymore. I have the creeping feeling that I could be arrested at any time. I do not have to do anything illegal, even an innuendo can send me away.

"First, there are the people at the market. You know how market women gossip. They have seen me find extra food for us and talk to people they do not know. They could alert the spies at any moment.

"Second involves with my friend, Herr Kübel, the hatter. He has hidden his father for years behind a false door in his apartment. The poor man has lived there this whole time as a 'submarine.' I know you got upset when you went to see Herr Kübel and he told you not to visit anymore. He only wanted to protect you. Being half Jewish, he is deathly afraid that he will be picked up any moment. Kübel Sr. recently started going for secret walks at three in the morning. Someone could have recognized him!

"Now, should anything happen to me, remember my driver, Franz Binter. He might be able to drive the truck a little while longer. I have no hope that the truck will survive the fighting. You and I are bound to get separated because you will not be able to avoid going off to fight with the Hitler Youth. This war cannot last more than a couple more months. Remember that we have a safe rallying point with Mother in Aigen-Schlägl. This year will not be a good one. As for the Russian atrocities in East Prussia, I hope it will not be as bad here. There is a good chance that the Americans will get to Mother first, so she should be safe."

I go to school the next day and find that all classes are suspended indefinitely.

Am I going to lose a whole school year?

My draft notice arrives because, unfortunately in this case, the mail is still working. I must report for service at our Hitler Youth station in two days. I have heard about Hitler Youth fighting on the front lines in Breslau and Berlin.

Do I have to go? Yes. Do I want to go? No, not really, but at least all my friends will also be there. If I do not go, the repercussions will be bad for me and my family.

Father says, "Fredi, do not tell anybody that you have Planneralm military training. If they hear that, they will put you in positions where you will be in even more danger. Do not let on that you can take your rifle apart or shoot well. And first and foremost, do not volunteer for anything. This war is lost; maybe it will all be over in a month. Do not get yourself killed. You are my only son and I need you."

I wish I could say something positive, but he is absolutely right. It makes me feel very close to him.

"Do not worry about Aunt Ria and I starving. I have squirrelled away enough food to sustain us for a couple of months."

Aunt Ria and Father are very afraid that they will never see me again. The worst part is that, at this time when my father really needs me most, I have to leave. l hope that at the end of this nightmare, we will be united again. Leaving them is not easy.

After transferring from the local Hitler Youth headquarters, our group —the boys from my neighbourhood, including Otto—are billeted at the former home of the Vienna Choir Boys.

"Elegant," Otto says. "If I could sing, I would feel like a choir boy."

"It is not your singing that is the problem, Otto. You are too ugly for them!"

Nice beds. We do not get the boys' linens, but blankets will do. There is a kitchen and good soup for us. We even have showers! Our unit is led by our regular local Hitler Youth leaders, boys only a year or two older than us. As there are no army officers available, orders come from within the Hitler Youth ranks itself. At this point, nobody is informing us about much of anything.

One of the rooms acts as our armoury. There are stacks of 89k rifles, a pile of Italian Beretta rifles and even a Sturmgewehr, which does not work. There is no ammunition for the Barettas. I receive an 89k, an army belt, a mess kit, a knapsack, a field flask, and a cartridge holder with twenty rounds. No helmets or bayonets. I am happy about that, though. There is already too much stuff to carry.

"Look at me, decorated like a Christmas tree."

We have to keep a twenty four hour guard on the building, one boy stationed at the entry on a four hour rotation. We are one small section of a single unit out of the thousands of boys that form the Vienna Hitler Youth. I have no idea where the other units are or what their orders are.

Our first task seems to be to control the streets of the inner city.

Since I do not hold any rank due to my previous lack of eagerness, I do not have any idea where we are going or what we are going to do. I just slog along. We are off for our first sortie.

"Watch out. Never let your guard down."

We walk in a stretched-out line, past all sorts of bomb damage. It is quiet along the Josefstädterstrasse. About fifty metres from Palais Auersperg, there are two loud explosions.

Pang, pang

"Is that our artillery?"

Debris falls from a house further up the street, and there is some smoke.

"Is that incoming Russian?"

"Can they be that close already?"

When we reach the Ringstrasse, three Tiger tanks with infantry crouched on top of them roar past us. All of the public buildings are damaged—some just pockmarked, some quite badly.

On the opposite side of the street, a company of infantry marches in a long, single file in the opposite direction. They are army regulars, many of them very young, but not as young as us.

Returning to the Choir Boys home, I just have time to get a bite to eat before it is time to pull my first, four hour round of guard duty.

"Halt! Who goes there? Password?"

"Mariahilf."

"Pass."

It sounds like overkill, but it keeps you awake.

The next day, we get up early. All the city's Hitler Youth units are to assemble at the Ministry of War. We march along, appalled by the state of such famous buildings as City Hall and the museums.

“Otto, look at the state of the Opera! All that rubble and chaos down on Kärtnerstrasse!”

Reaching the Ministry, we all assemble in a giant formation, ten rows deep. The regional leader of the Vienna Hitler Youth addresses us.

“Comrades, The Fatherland is in great peril. We call on you to give your utmost, even your life, in its defence. Today you will be given the honour of swearing an oath of obedience to our Führer and Reichskanzler, Adolf Hitler.”

Otto is standing next to me in line.

“How can we get out of this?” I whisper.

“I do not know. Do not let any of the others hear you. If they make you say your name, just say Mayer instead of Penz. And cross your fingers, that makes it void.”

I did not have to say my name, but I did cross my fingers.

The sound of the National Anthem is always moving. After that, the Horst-Wessel-Lied, the Third Reich’s ditty, sounds trivial. I think about Dr. Trnka’s lecture about the Mayas sacrificing young boys on the altar of their gods.

Our days at the Choir Boys home are numbered. This morning, twenty of us are taken to the head of Simmeringer Hauptstrasse, a broad street leading south, to deal with some trouble. As we arrive, there is a great surprise, twenty bicycles! We are now a bicycle patrol. Due to my congenital balance problems, all my previous attempts at cycling have ended badly. I do not know what to do, so I tell the boys about my dilemma.

“What are we going to do with this guy?”

So the unit’s main objective is no longer intercepting enemy incursions but teaching Alfred Penz how to master the bicycle. The success of our venture is dependent on it. They run beside me, holding me and the bicycle, but every time they let go, I fall over like a Christmas tree spilling all my military ornaments. After about three-quarters of an hour, they get me to a point where I can wiggle along as they support and encourage me.

Horror!

Two Yak-2 Russian bombers appear above us, turning for an attack. Everyone scrambles to the side of the road, taking cover in doorways wherever they can. I wiggle along, dead centre of the road, more afraid of my bicycle than the planes. When I glance up, I see the first bomber coming directly at me. I see muzzle fire at its wings.

Tzzziiink – Tzzziiink – Tzzziiink – Tzzziiink
Tzzziiink – Tzzziiink – Tzzziiink – Tzzziiink – Tzzziiink – Tzzziiink

Slugs hit the pavement around me, sparks and granite splinters strike me. Still, I wiggle along on the bicycle. Then the second fighter comes. More muzzle fire at the wings, but this plane is shooting behind me. I stop my bicycle, falling to the ground.

WHAM

A vehicle bursts into flame ten metres behind me. The person who gets out of it is a burning torch. I lie entwined in that damned bicycle and all my gear, stunned. I move my arm. Thank God, I am still alive. The boys come back and stand above me.

"Fredi, we thought you were dead."

"You are alive!"

Yes, I am alive, but the patrol is dead. In the end, that did not really matter. We get to the pickup place in time and leave the bicycles at the designated spot. When we get back to our base, we find out that other things are more pressing now. We hardly sleep. This will be the last night that we enjoy the hospitality of the Choir Boys home.

Alarm. It is two in the morning.

"Assignment! Get dressed and grab your gear."

The Russians are at Laaer Berg, a hill south of the city.

Do they expect us to stop them?

Tense and apprehensive, we climb up onto the platforms of two trucks, off for our first real battle assignment. Rumbling through the night, the sounds of war intensify.

Mixed feelings.

Are we going to be alive tomorrow?

We are still very young and, as far as battle experience goes, as green as frogs. We are scared but not cowardly. It is the uncertainty, the lack of experience. Marching around in formation does not make you a soldier. We are facing battle-hardened soldiers with years of experience on the front. When the trucks stop, the noise gets louder—infantry fire from just a few streets away. It is very dark. We cannot see further than two metres in front of us.

After a couple of blocks, a lieutenant and two soldiers receive us, standing in front of what looks like a giant garbage disposal made from pieces of destroyed vehicles, with the whole facade of a three-story house spread across the street.

"Heil Hitler, men!"

"Heil Hitler, Herr Lieutenant!"

He explains the situation to our leader. "The Russians have several patrols of five to ten men behind our lines to reconnoitre and cause confusion. This barricade, or whatever you want to call it, will defer them. Since there are about twenty of you, you can stop them by hiding behind the junk. Should there be a tank, we have three Panzer-fausts for you. Good luck, men."

Man the barricade? What barricade?

Our leader inspects the barricade and assigns small groups to guard different parts of the obstacle course. It is a horrible night, the ultimate blackout, flash-lit only by exploding artillery shells. We learned to distinguish the sound of Russian machine pistols from the chainsaw-like bursts of our MG 42s.

Our barricade is just a junkyard, starting at the ruins of a destroyed house and running to a point where it is just wide enough to allow a vehicle passage. It consists of tons of rubble, topped by smashed furniture and God knows what else. Finding appropriate cover, with the necessary field to fire from, is a conundrum, but somehow we manage.

About twenty boys stretch from the lowest point to right up inside the house. For about an hour, we rummage around, moving garbage, furniture parts, mortar blocks, and generally getting in each other's hair. Pepi, our leader, has the good idea to split us up.

Finally, we are settled, shivering from fear, fright, and fatigue, straining to see in the dark. Then—

Crack, crack, crack, crack

Bullets stab into the garbage. The Russians are here. In the dark, I see a shadow moving. I take aim, fire, take aim, and fire again. A flare climbs above us. Its glaring light floats down on a little parachute, flooding the barricade with bright light and causing us to freeze into a bizarre tableau.

Another hail of bullets. Then nothing. The light is no more. We slump, panting. No matter how few they are, they can easily overwhelm us with their firepower. But nothing happens. Quiet. There is neither sight nor sound of any Russians. They seem to have withdrawn. Shivering and fighting sleep, we are in a stupor—leaning, laying, and hanging onto the tangle of refuse.

Franz Janucek says, "Image someone coming by this heap of crap and seeing you lying face down on this. 'Look what I found?' he'd say."

At about five in the morning, another officer arrives, telling us that we are being relieved. The trucks will pick us up and take us to another mission. Hurray! We have won the battle of the garbage heap! No one can say that we never fired a shot. We march several hundred metres to the rear where trucks are ready to take us to an unknown destination.

What was this? I wonder. *What was the sense of it? Was it just an appetizer of war to prepare us for the main course?*

I remember the sergeant at the Planneralm. Never try to understand an order, just obey it.

We are dropped off at what appears to be a university research building. It was badly hit. The room where we spend the remainder of the night is littered with broken glassware. We use boards to clear areas of broken glass so that we can try to snatch a couple of hours of sleep on the floor.

In the morning, still under the spell of the previous day, we stumble hungry, thirsty, and dishevelled out of the ruined building to find trucks waiting for us again. We are given some bread, some porridge ladled out of thermal buckets, and water.

Back on the trucks, we are ferried to the Ministry of War. It is now defence headquarters. Other groups of boys arrive. In the end, we total well over a hundred. We assemble in formation inside the courtyard. Two photographers and a film cameraman from the propaganda ministry are reconnoitring to find the best light and positions.

A Hitler Youth Stammführer addresses us. "Comrades, we are assembled to thank you for your bravery in action. We are proud to see the embodiment of the German youth in you, in your power to resist the onslaught from the east. Reichskommissar, Baldur von Schirach, will now address you."

There he is. One of the uppermost stars in the National Socialist firmament is to thank us in person. He walks among the ranks, shaking hands and addressing individual boys. Walking right past me, he shakes Otto's hand, closely followed by the camera people.

"Otto, you will be a star at the Wochenschau (the weekly film showing at all the cinemas)."

And then he stands in front of us all.

"Comrades, another heroic period in the history of your city has begun. You have the honour to become…"

WHAM

A bomb whizzes above us.

Tssk, tssk, tssk, tssk
WHAM

Another bomb explodes.

A group of fighter planes is attacking the building like a swarm of angry hornets, firing their cannons and dropping bombs.

Mid-sentence, he says, "Wegtreten!" (dismissed) and heads for the safety of the building's interior with us right behind him.

The propaganda ministry people have stopped filming.

The Russians are in the city.

Coming from the south, via Simmering, they are in the Third and Fourth Districts. We get the news from passing troops. I am terribly afraid for the safety of my family. I am glad that they are not at the edge of the Gürtel, which could easily become a defence line. Aunt Poldi's apartment overlooks the green space there.

We are in limbo again.

If you do not know what to do with a military unit, move them.

Many troops in the city are not under central command. Every day there is another general in command, sometimes two at once.

We are on patrol. The destruction is depressing. There are many barricades in the city, some unsecured. There is so much debris, one would need a tank to get by it all. There is no sign of the two SS Panzer Divisions, whatever is left of them, that retreated from Hungary.

Rumour has it that Ivan has captured the Schottenring and reached the canal. We hear that there were stocks of Panzerfausts on both sides of the canal and now Ivan and the SS are duelling with them across the canal.

Are we going to be trapped on the south shore of the Danube?

It crosses my mind that being a deserter and hiding at home might be safer.

The Steffl, St. Stephen's Cathedral is burning. Flames shoot through its roof, which collapses. Most of the Graben and all the area around the Dom is in flames. The Pummerin, St. Stephen's giant bell—cast from the metal of Turkish cannons—thunders through its base. There goes the symbol of Vienna.

Will it ever be rebuilt?

We see the fire in the city centre even from a distance.

We cross the Aspernbrücke, moving through the Josefstadt. Wherever we turn, there is smoke from incoming artillery fire. We pass a small group of army and SS men preparing to counterattack. They tell us the Russians have crossed the Rotundenbrücke in force.

We are on Praterstrasse, marching toward the Reichsbrücke (Imperial bridge). Passing the Praterstern Train Station, we encounter Dante's Inferno.

On our left, all of the coal slides of the Railway Freight Terminal are on fire. Flames leap high, spreading smoke and heat.

On our right, the entire Prater Amusement Park is an enormous conflagration, spreading heat and sucking the oxygen out of the air. The giant Ferris wheel is taking its last dying turn, all its cars aflame. All the lovely rides—the ghost train, the panorama ride, etc—send columns of flame skyward. The Big Dipper collapses. Our childhood heaven condemned to a blazing hell.

Silhouetted against this deadly conflagration, a shadowy stream of desperation. Axis troops of all colours are anxious to cross the bridge safely. It will be blown up any minute.

"Stay together. Build groups of three so nobody falls behind. Watch out for each other. We do not want anyone left behind!"

Horrified, scared, we first pass single corpses and then a heap of horror—a tangle of Croat soldiers who were Kalashnikov'd from behind. A loud ongoing scream—the same four Slavic words—goes on and on. A head, eyes popping, mouth gaping and distorted in lethal terror. A throat ripped like a slaughtered pig. A crimson rivulet meanders between the cobbles. A trooper's brain is blown out and spread across his face. A lieutenant left behind, covered in blood, is trying to stop a comrade's gushing blood, using his belt as a tourniquet.

"Go, go, go! No time for sightseeing!"

"Get your asses moving!"Running, panting, falling, we see Hungarian Arrow Cross units, Slovak and Croat troops, and civilians. In between, Russian patrols fire at everyone in sight. Some soldiers carry the wounded piggyback, stop and go. Retreating SS troops fire at the Russian. At the bridge's edge, two giant bombs, the largest I could have ever imagined, wait to be detonated.

A group of pioneers stand by, waiting for the order. As long as these men are standing there, she is not going to blow. The sight of the bombs makes us break into a jog. At the far end of the bridge, two more of the same bombs wait.

"Hurray, we are across!"

Getting a few hundred metres further away makes everyone sigh in relief. Then the anticlimax sets in. That was one hell of an escape. Everyone breathes deeply as we rest for a few minutes on the side of the road, watching the stream of escapees pass by and waiting for the big bang. The enormous bombs sit on the bridge, ready to explode, but no bang.

Are they ever going to blow up the bridge?

Marching along Wagramerstrasse, we pass the Old Danube, a side branch of the main river artificially created in the late 1800s. The moon has come out and shimmers on the water. The war now feels like the rumble of a distant thunderstorm.

"Otto, look. On the left, the Gänsehäufel! What a treat it was to go swimming there with the family."

Will that ever happen again?

We are marching, dragging ourselves west to reach Floridsdorf. At the Floridsdorferstrasse, we meet Hitler Youth who were in action in another part of the city. They are in horrible shape, having been involved in heavy fighting. Hundreds dead and wounded. They are totally wiped out, some bandaged. They were attacking the Russians. They just came across the Floridsdorferbrücke and say it is still intact.

We hear about Major Biedermann and two of his adjutants hanging on signposts at the Floridsdorferbrücke with 'I negotiated with the enemy' signs around their necks. Three Viennese who gave their lives for love of their city.

We enter a school, collapse on the floor of the gymnasium, and pass out. The events of the day have exhausted us.

A giant monster made of whirling clouds has a man in his claws, bites his head off, and squeezes out the blood. Its other claw comes down on me.

"Arshrrr!!!"

"Fredi! Fredi! Wake up, you had a nightmare."

"Get up! Get up! We have to get out of here!"

I have a headache; every part of my body hurts.

There is fighting going on not far from us. The now familiar noises of the front—the blast of bombs, the rattle of machine-gun fire, the burst of artillery shells.

Are they across the Floridsdorferbrücke? Is it not blown up? What happened at the Reichsbrücke, did they not explode those giant bombs?

Those huge bombs surely must have brought it down by now, we reason. Anyway, they are on our side of the river and there could be a T-34 in front of the door any minute. We gulp water like horses, splash our faces, and are out of the door. No T-34. Instead a Tiger tank and SS infantry—a reception committee on the north shore for Ivan. That should give us time to get out of the way.

There are no orders for us. At this point, we are numb. What happens, happens. I am glad that our immediate leaders are guided by common sense. They have no heroic ideas of attacking the Russians. The road is full of soldiers—some moving one way, some the other.

Has the command structure broken down? The supply train scattered?

There are no final orders and no food. Every unit scavenges for its own supplies. Communications are disrupted. All units move as isolated islands, reacting to the enemy. The cold air and the diminishing war are a bit relaxing. Getting out of the northern reaches of Vienna, we pass Korneuburg and march on to Stockerau. No sign of the foe.

After the massive flight to the west from Eastern Germany, we expect big numbers of refugees on the road, but no. Not here in Austria. As my father said, you are safer in your own house, safer in a large city. That might not hold true, however, in places where you might be lynched by your own, such as the Ustaše in Croatia.

There is no sign of the enemy except for three Russian planes heading west, flying high above us. Marching into Stockerau, we encounter quite a few SS troopers from Sepp Dietrich's Das Reich SS Panzer Division. Part of it must be here on the north shore. Pepi Janitchek's brother serves in it.

Would it not be great if he could see him?

We sleep on the floor of an empty store west of Stockerau. It is better than sleeping outside on the ground.

"Can the upper leadership keep track of us here or are we now dependent on charity?"

After some hints from our leader, the SS came through with a small donation. Each of us receives a third of a loaf of hard army bread and a third of a can of beef. For the bread, we have our teeth and our Hitler Youth daggers to cut through it. For the canned beef, we form groups of three and open one can a day. Dinner solved for 3 days. The beef is pretty awful, especially eaten cold. We crave the protein though and remember what they say about looking a gift horse in the mouth.

The new boots which Father scrounged for me are too small. My feet are killing me. Grandfather, Father, and I have the same large feet. Shoes in size 56 are rare. Grandfather had his shoes custom-made, but that is just a dream these days.

We stay overnight at a school. I do not know what kind of school it is, but it has showers that still run hot water. We really stink. We have not washed since the Choir Boys home. We will have to put up with the same dirty underwear and socks. Their odour is disgusting and even the holes have holes. Despite the short duration and the lack of soap, the flow of hot water over my body feels heavenly. Despite the hard floor, I fall into a deep sleep.

Wham

An explosion nearby. Some of us rush the door to see.

"Go back to sleep, boys," an SS man sitting on a BMW motorcycle says. "It was just a sewing machine."

Our soldiers call these outmoded Soviet biplanes 'sewing

machines' because their engines sound like one. They fly high overhead at night. If they see any light, they switch off their engines and glide down to drop one or two bombs. Their effect is mainly psychological.

"Go back to sleep."

In the morning we are back on the move again. We note more and more SS along the road. They are not moving; some are in defensive positions. On the market square, a lot of soldiers and locals are talking.

"The Führer is dead," a loudspeaker mounted on top of a command truck repeats over and over. "Today, at ten in the morning, our Führer and Reichskanzler left his command bunker and joined soldiers defending a barricade. He was killed by enemy fire. His successor will be Grand Admiral Karl Dönitz who is in Flensburg. He will speak to you shortly."

Stunned silence. This is a monumental moment in the Reich's history. For most, their God is dead. They have sacrificed five of their best years on his altar, and for millions their very lives. For the heretics, there remains only the frightening question, 'What happens now?'

As we walk, we meet more and more SS troops sitting in and on their vehicles by the wayside.

"How are you, boys?"

They are very fatherly to us, maybe because many of them are fathers to boys and girls our age. They are pleasant but guarded. Our unit leader learns that a highly decorated lieutenant was tried by summary court-martial and shot for saying, "Boys, go home before you get killed." The verdict: condemned for Zersetzung der Wehrkraft (diminishing martial energy). For us, for now, the war must go on. Westward we go, or is it northwest?

"Cover! Yak-2 bombers!"

We scramble for cover. I crouch behind a spindly tree. There he is, coming right at me. I have my rifle up, firing at the pilot. I see his muzzle fire. I was aiming at him, but he was not aiming at me.

There are soldiers behind us. None were hurt, but one slug hit the back of their truck. Further on, a cow barn is starting to burn. Tracer bullets have set the roof ablaze. We are ordered to go help if we can. We shed our gear and leave one boy to guard it. A terrified, crazed cow passes us, screaming as I have never heard a cow scream before.

Soldiers nearby have already arrived to help the farmer get his animals out of the stable. They manage to get most of the animals out but sadly not all. A large blaze shoots upwards. A ceiling of fire forms with a void underneath. Very strange looking. It is very, very hot.

No one can go near the barn anymore. The back of the family's home is now threatened by the flames. Our task now is to help the woman, neighbours, and soldiers move valuables and furniture out of the home via a hand-to-hand chain.

The volunteer fire department arrives. They deploy an antique water pump, shooting a stream of water on the house. It is a type of see-saw, manual pump. Two men on each side pump up and down to force water through the hose to help cool the building. After a while, the barn is just a heap of embers, but the house is out of danger. Things are under control, except for all the cows wandering around in the dark.

We are ordered to return to where we were before, to get some rest. The good part is that no human lives were lost, but I feel sad for the animals.

On our march westward, we receive orders to form a defensive line on a specific hill. Since we only have road maps, we are not too sure where we are. It must be the hill on our left.

Some of us are ordered to take position on the lower part of the hill. The rest will be on the top of the hill, with our headquarters in a semi-underground storage building. I am assigned as messenger between the two positions. Presently, I am at the lower position.

"Jesus, Russians! See them up the road there? Three, four, about ten. Down below. Right behind those bushes next to the road? They are moving towards us. Go tell the others. Quickly!"

I rise and move as fast as I can up the slope.

Pluck, pluck, pluck, pluck

Bullets slam into the grass, only a metre to the left of me. A high-voltage lighting bolt hits my brain.

I am dead.

Instinctively, I turn and jump over the impacts.

Pluck, pluck, pluck, pluck

Impacts hit where I was before.

Zigzag?

My mind already feels the deadly, piercing slugs in my body. But suddenly, surprise, quiet. No more shots. I cannot believe it. I am alive and unhurt. I stumble into the command post.

"There are Russians below our lower position. They nearly killed me!"

But they are not there any longer. They have disappeared. Possibly just a reconnaissance unit. Our hill gives us a commanding view of the opposing valley.

Peering through the only pair of binoculars between us all, our unit leader says, "Jesus. There are two Vienna fire trucks and a large group of Vienna city policemen forming some sort of defence position. They have a truck loaded with Panzerfausts."

They, like us, seemed to be armed only with 89k rifles. There is no military paraphernalia dangling from their belts. Like us, they have no spades to dig in with.

“By God, what are the fireman doing here?”

They firemen are huddled behind two of the department’s best fire engines, ones equipped with ladders that can reach four stories up. They appear unarmed.

“Why would they bring those expensive fire engines up here?”

“In the long run, the Russians would have gotten them anyway. One way or another.”

Further up the field, hidden by trees and bushes, an armoured Russian personnel carrier is waiting. Its machine gun and cannon could make mincemeat out of an ad hoc defence force that probably has even less military training than we do.

We see them all leave. First, the Russian vehicle disappears. Then the fire engines and the police pack up and head westward. Suddenly, there are no fire engines, no policemen, and no Russians. They have all vanished, disappearing like spooky phantoms.

We are marching again, westward, to become part of the Alpenfestung (Alpine Fortress), the last stand.

Orders are orders; we trudge along. Again, we see no refugees. People feel safer staying put. Whatever happens, happens. Better at home than on the open road. We pass several villages untouched by war. My feet hurt from the blisters.

“What do you think our leaders are planning?”

“Do they want to repeat history’s heroic last stands?”

Wanderer, as you pass for Sparta, tell them you have seen us laying here as the law ordered.

“Well, then they fought with swords and spears. Now, you need tanks, ammunition, and fuel.”

“I guess even with the Führer dead, some of the upper-ups cannot face the fact that we have lost,” I say.

“Fredi, do not ever use the word ‘lost.’ That can still get you shot.”

One foot in front of the other. One foot in front of the other. The further we get from the fighting, the less we see of the civilian population. We pass a village. It feels like passing through a ghost town. Two dogs are on the street. They do not even bark. The people are hiding.

Marching would not be so bad without all the military hardware we have to carry. The heaviest thing is the 89k carbine, that relic of the First World War. And then the water bottle, food bag, and cartridge holder. At least we do not carry any Panzerfausts with us.

"You know that the regular army boots, the Knobelbechers (the dice cups), are better for marching than any of our boots," I complain. "And these rags for socks…."

"Yes, for us, but not for you. You can be sure they do not have your size."

There is a working water fountain in the middle of the next village. Great for filling our flasks and splashing our faces. At the end of the village, we finally meet another living person—a very old man with a sloppy hat and a leather apron. He has left his task to see us pass.

"Good luck, boys. God bless you."

No, 'Heil Hitler.'

The kilometres drag on.

"What do they mean by sending us to the Alpine Fortress? We are several hundred kilometres away from any mountains. Are they seriously going to have us walk there?"

We reach another hamlet but can only guess where we are because they have removed all the signs at the village entrance—as if the Russians could read them anyway. At a rest stop, Walter Berry and I hear our names called.

"Come with us."

A group is assembled around two figures, sitting frightened on the ground.

"These two were caught spying on us through these bushes. They have what appears to be Russian road maps on them with all kinds of cryptic writing. If the SS get them, they stand no chance, but there could be something to all these notations. You two shall escort them to the nearest police station. Since we have no vehicle, you will accomplish that by stopping military vehicles and asking them for a ride."

We motion for the two suspects to rise and come with us. They wear the typical Eastern peasant attire of baggy clothes. I try a few Czech words. They do not seem to be Slavic or Hungarian. Both are very sombre and dirty. The younger one seems to be around thirty, the older one about fifty. We have their maps. They carry their knapsacks which contain some utensils, raw potatoes, and other vegetables. They must have been living off the land for some time.

The unit will meet up with us at an army barracks at the Pyhrn Pass, two hundred kilometres south of Linz.

I do not like leaving the boys. I haven't even had a chance to say goodbye to Otto, but an order is an order. Our captives seem harmless. We move to the road and see our unit march off, waving at us.

Our strange little group stands next to the road, waving at army vehicles. First, a convoy of eight vehicles—a motorcycle, a command car, and six trucks—slows down. An officer in the lead car shouts an explanation at us as it rolls on. The next vehicle's destination is only a kilometre up the road, but they stop anyway and talk to us. The third one, a three-ton Opel Blitz, stops.

"We are going all the way to Linz. If you want to come with us, you can ride in the back."

We clamber up the platform, giving the older captive a hand up. We sit amid a load of ammunition boxes and some gasoline canisters. We have won the lottery. About five kilometres on, we pass our unit slogging along.

"Look at the freeloaders."

"All the best. See you in heaven!"

I feel bad for my friends, my brothers in arms, but we won the ride, and orders are orders. It becomes obvious that all the fighting is happening south of the Danube. We stop at another village fountain. Three soldiers get out of the cab.

"Get some water, boys. You want some bread?"

There are some locals about, but cautious, they keep a safe distance. We are now a ways from the war. No Soviet aircraft. Our captives wolf down the bread and gulp the water. One of our soldiers gives them two empty beer bottles to fill with water. Without stoppers, they have to hold them upright. They are very glum and dejected, not saying a word, not even to each other.

We ride past horrible figures, staggering, stumbling, laying along the road. Living skeletons in worn, striped tunics. Inmates from the Mauthausen concentration camp. The guards must have fled and now these living dead are out, hoping to reach salvation. By the state of the ones we see, I wonder how many are still inside, too weak to move.

A good many of these walking corpses are political prisoners. I know the camps are there; we are often threatened with them. Toe the line, or off you go to die. I recognize the Pöstlingberg mountain. We cross the Nibelungenbrücke. Looking down onto the Danube, we notice quite a bit of damage along the shore and a sunken steamer. Arriving at the Landstrasse in Linz, the truck stops.

"Is this alright for you?"

"Thank you very much for the ride."

We clamber over the side of the truck, our two prisoners behind us. The truck drives off.

"Good luck, boys!"

We stand in the middle of the Landstrasse which is as wide as a square. Linz is a very pretty town, the provincial capital of Oberdonau (Upper Austria). The old town, with its narrow streets, is very picturesque. This is the town where Hitler spent most of his teen years.

“Can you please tell us where we can find a police station?”

Following instructions, our little group trudges along. The two captives have said very little to each other and never attempted to communicate with us. How easily these two could have overwhelmed us, even with the three soldiers in the cab. Maybe they really are just a couple of displaced peasants.

Entering the police station, we find the place in a state of chaos. Every drawer and filing cabinet is open. Heaps of paper everywhere. There is smoke; something is burning.

“Heil Hitler, we are Vienna Hitler Youth. We have been ordered to deliver these two men to the nearest police station.”

We hand over the maps and describe the circumstances. The officer, a man of about fifty, looks at the two.

“The war has displaced millions of people. These two look pretty harmless. We will keep them here for a day. The Americans are going to be here soon, anyway.”

We try to say goodbye to the prisoners. They respond with the same stoic faces.

Standing outside the station, I say, “What now?”

Walter has an aunt in Bad Hall, and I have family fifty kilometres north of here in Aigen-Schlägl.

“My career as a singer is my life. I can live out the last days of this war with my aunt. Bad Hall will be ideal for weathering the end of the war. All this exercise has been dangerous for me. I could have lost my voice!”

“The boys will need a few more days to reach the Spital and the Pyhrn Pass barracks.”

“What are you going to do if you go see your family?” he asks. “Will you stay there for good?”

“I am definitely going to visit my mother and my new sister unless the Americans beat me there and block me.”

“Well, good luck. I will see you after the war is over.”

“And I hope that when I see you next, you will be on stage at the rebuilt Vienna State Opera.”

"Servus Fredi."

"Servus Walter."

He heads west. I head north.

There is little damage on the Landstrasse. A cool breeze on the bridge makes me feel at peace. If only I was not lugging all this military paraphernalia. The way to the Mühlkreis Railway Station is comfortably familiar. The grand old lady sits there like an 1890 museum exhibit. Unfortunately, she stopped operating yesterday. I am dead broke, not a Pfennig.

Would they have taken me for free?

But that is no longer relative. The road north runs parallel to the tracks for quite a distance. I wave at a passing Opel Blitz with a lone driver.

"Are you going to Aigen-Schlägl?"

"No, but I can take you for twenty kilometres. Then I head west." I climb into the cab, fumbling with rifle and gear.

"You are armed for war."

"Yeah, it is hard to carry all this crap with you."

"Where are you from?"

"Vienna."

"Been involved in the fighting?"

"Just had a taste of it."

"I am from Frankfurt, hauling gasoline for my outfit. Even all those jerry cans in the back are not as much as we need. No gas, no ammunition, no food. Well, it will be over soon. That will be good for you, too. You have not even started to really live yet."

He turns left onto a side road. I have to go north.

"Good luck."

"Thanks for the ride."

I walk along, hoping for a lift. Then a roar. A twin-bodied aircraft at very low altitude screams at high speed over me, rises into a turn, and descends for attack, firing its cannons.

Tak, tak, tak, tak, tak, tak, tak, tak
Bang, bang, bang

My God, my new friend's jerry cans!

BANG BANG BANG
WHAM WHAM WHAM WHAM

Explosions and billowing black smoke. I sit down, feeling sick, and retch. This damned war.

A single vehicle, some kind of personnel carrier, with an officer and two soldiers in the cab stops.

"Where are you going soldier?"

"Aigen-Schlägl."

"We can drop you off right in the middle of the town. We are going to Ulrichsberg further up. Hop in."

The eight SS men in the back are friendly.

"Where are you from?"

"Vienna."

"We, except the officer, are from the Banat. All recruited into the SS, not voluntarily."

"Just over a year ago, I was on KLV with my school in the Vojvodina. It seems so long ago."

The vehicle stops a block from my grandfather's house. He is a prominent citizen in Aigen-Schlägl.

"Fredi, good to see you alive!"

Most people in the town know me, since this is my childhood

summer home. Aunt Margret is just leaving the house. My grandmother is sitting at the alcove. With two large windows in front of her, she can see who is walking by outside. She has an extreme case of gout, which causes her legs to swell terribly. She is in constant pain.

"Fredi, you are here! You are alive! Your mother and new sister are out for a walk with the pram."

Mother's family members arrive and finally my mother with my new sister.

"Fredi, Fredi, Fredi! I am so glad to see you!"

Mother gives me a long, long hug. I hold my sister for the first time. She is so little, so frail. I do not even know how to hold a baby. Unfortunately, this peace is just a blip.

Aunt Margret's husband explains the situation. "Fredi, I hate to say this, but you are not safe here. We still have many party faithful that would turn you over to the SS. There is fighting at Schwarzenberg and the retreating SS are dangerous. The Americans could arrive here in days, too.

"You have two options. Tonight, we can throw all your gear into the garden pond, find you some clothes, and hide you in the attic. Or you go back to your unit and await the end of the war there."

In perhaps the stupidest thing I have ever done, I decide to go back to the boys. I have a nice meal and a bath, get new underwear and sleep for a few hours in a proper bed. The next morning, I hear the sounds that I know so well—the sounds of war.

After kissing my distraught family goodbye, I climb into my uncle's car. He lets me out about five kilometres south.

"I have to let you go here, otherwise I might not make it back to Aigen-Schlägl."

On the road again. On the long way back to friends who might already have marched as far as the Pyhrn Pass. I now face even more danger. The military police are hunting for deserters. These bullies, called 'chain dogs' for the metal Militärpolizei plates hanging around their neck, are famous for instant executions.

It is a long way south. After walking a couple of kilometres, a car driven by two uniformed party officials of high-rank stops.

"Where are you going, soldier?"

"I am rejoining my unit at the Pyhrn Pass. We will be in position then to defend the Alpine Fortress."

"Alright, comrade."

I climb in the back of their Mercedes and ask, "How far are you going?"

"About fifty kilometres south of Linz. Where are you from?"

"Vienna, we defended the city."

How much luck can one boy have?

I hope they do not ask any further questions. Luckily, they are occupied debating something. We pass through Linz. This was my most critical point and the most difficult stretch to reach. They continue to ignore me, too busy talking. They stop at Wels.

"We are going to let you out here. We go by the main road. This road will lead you to the Pyhrn Pass, via Windischgarten."

I am standing along the roadside again. The sky is overcast; it looks like it is going to rain. There is quite a bit of traffic, most of it army convoys going south to defend the Alpine Fortress.

Do I want to take a last stand?

Crazy as it is, I just want to see my friends. Only single vehicles ever stop to pick up stragglers. Convoys never do. An army unit marches past me, about a company strong. I sit on a rock, resting, and watch them head south toward the pass. The war rumbles in the distance.

"Got lost, soldier?" A truck stops, two soldiers in the cab.

"Heading to Pyhrn Pass, to join my unit."

"So are we. Hop in." He sees me notice the approximately twenty gasoline cans on the deck behind us. "The whole army is out of gas."

I am very nervous about the freight riding behind me. I do not want to be incinerated.

"We support a Panzer reconnaissance unit. They are on the other south side of the pass, totally out of gas."

One of the men is from Frankfurt, the other one from Heidelberg.

"Out of fuel and out of ammunition."

"The Americans have total control of the air now. We have no more aviation fuel, so all the pilots have been transferred to the infantry."

Speak of the devil. Their roaring engines petrify me. An enemy fighter screams over us but pays us no attention, heading for the pass. As we pass towns, we notice civilians boarding up windows.

Where did they get the wood? Are they tearing up their white sheets to turn them into flags?

We are passed by more troops heading south. Off the road, an abandoned Tiger tank sits in a field like a dead dinosaur—its cannon pointing to the sky, its hatches open.

At the side of the road, a school bus full of young girls and a priest in a cassock appears stranded. A person under the hood is trying to fix it. He gets out from under the hood and waves at us for help. My driver doesn't stop. I think he is nervous about the gasoline.

A small, high-wing command plane hums over us like a bee looking for nectar.

Is it getting to know us?

We are definitely dealing with Americans now, not the Russians. I harbour no bad feelings against the Russians, as a people. They have suffered more than anybody from this steamroller of a war rolling back and forth over their country.

We reach Spital, the town at the base of the pass.

"Good luck finding your unit!"

"Good luck to you, too. Do not get yourself killed!"

"Have you seen a group of teenagers marching up the pass?"

"Yes, they are at the barracks near the summit."

It is past noon now, and I am pooped. The steep slope does not help. A kilometre up, a first lieutenant comes towards me. He is very young and wears the medical insignia.

"Are you on your way to join the boys at the barracks on the top of the hill?"

"I am."

"Do not go up there. The place is dangerously in chaos."

I learn that more than half of the boys have dropped out and are headed for relatives. The rest are threatened by a small group of fanatics who talk about fighting to the death. They murdered a boy named Haberl and are threatening everybody else. I remember Haberl. He used to attend the Humanist gymnasium (high school) on Amerlingstrasse.

"As you can see, I am your unit's junior medical officer. If asked, you have not met me."

Hallelujah. I have found my guardian angel. He will help me out of this mess that I have gotten myself into. My new friend is Dr. Karl Kerner. He was a hospital intern in Tegernsee, in Bavaria, when they drafted him. We cut a wide trail down the slope, staying away from any guards from the camp who might surprise us, and turn onto a narrow road.

"Look what we have here, a horse and buggy!"

We cautiously approach—not a soul in sight. The horse is tethered to a tree with the bit out of its mouth.

"Hello? Hello, anybody here?"

An empty pistol case is laying on the seat of the buggy, next to two suitcases and a carriage box.

"Herr Doctor?"

"For simplicity's sake, just call me Doctor. I will call you Fredi."

Examining the first suitcase, we find a party uniform in the usual feces-coloured brown with gold leaf on the collar.

"Pretty high-ranking guy."

"If the owner killed himself, which seems likely, he will not be hanging from a tree."

There is even a box containing food. Half a loaf of real rye bread, some Emmental cheese, real butter, and four bottles of beer. The doctor tries on a smart sports jacket. It is a little loose but that is the trend nowadays. There are shirts, socks, all kinds of grooming stuff, and a box with some money.

"Finders keepers. We will split the money."

"Are we not a pair of happy vultures?"

"Well, if we do not take it, someone else will."

The doctor looks smart in his new outfit. I discover a fur-collared olive jacket, which I fancy. The new underwear and socks feel fine. We strip the buggy of any incriminating trace of the Nazi. We can still hear the sounds of war in the distance. Infantry, but no heavy guns. SS moving up the pass, maybe.

"Listen, we have to take a break. Wait until noon, at least. There are still too many crazies around, like the ones at the barracks. Some would fight on even after an armistice."

I remember a little clearing further down, hidden by bushes.

"We will go there. It will hide the buggy."

The horse really likes having his bit exchanged for the bag of oats in the wagon. He really is lovely.

"What shall we name him?"

"Do not get attached to him. We will have to abandon him soon."

I name him Pepi, anyway. I lead Pepi down to a little creek at the bottom of the clearing and watch him drink water. I stroke him and put my face against his muzzle.

"Good boy, Pepi. I hope you survive all this, too."

We pull some blankets and enough other stuff from the buggy to make ourselves comfortable while we wait for noon, waiting for the war to be over. Considering everything, we both sleep well. To the Americans, we will just be more civilians without papers. Maybe. Should there be SS, the doctor is smart and eloquent enough to get us past them.

We reach the main road three or four kilometres south of Spital. Pandemonium. We merge into a maelstrom of German soldiers. We see our first Americans. Troops ride by in covered trucks led by officers in small square cars. Driving south, we ignore the herds of disarmed German soldiers stripped of their military gear, heading north to captivity. Some look dejected, some elated.

Germany has surrendered unconditionally.

"Hurray, the war is over. We are still alive!"

We reach the outskirts of Spital.

"From now on, we go on foot. It is less conspicuous."

"Do I have to part with Pepi?"

At a widening of the road, we undo the horse's bit and tie him to a fence. I stroke Pepi from cheek to muzzle.

"Goodbye, Pepi. I hope you make it."

As I walk away, I hear him whinny, an equine way of saying, "Servus Fredi."

We join the mass again—thousands of soldiers practically shoulder to shoulder.

"It is time for the two of us to split up, too."

"I hope you make it home to Tegernsee."

"Go see your mother and sister."

"Thank you, Doctor, for taking me under your wing."

"Do not mention it. Take care."

"Take care, Doctor."

The doctor disappears into the masses. I head for the Americans. Expect the unexpected. Only boldness will do the trick. I decide to ask an American officer for a ride north to my mother. I look young enough, and I am not in uniform. I have no papers, and spies are out of fashion. I was better at English than French, anyway.

"Good day. Can you please take me to Mister Kommander?"

Bemused, the sergeant says, "Bill, take the boy to the Colonel."

A hundred or so khaki-clad soldiers sit on the ground and in their vehicles, talking, laughing, and smoking. The war is over. The command post is a former police station. Several officers are grouped around a tall figure, the commander.

"Who is that boy?"

"Mister Commander,..." I say.

He has an idea. "You speak German?"

"Of course. I am Austrian, Mister Commander."

"This valley is crammed with thousands of prisoners. I need to know what their units were. Would you come on a walk with me and help me find out?"

Followed by a sergeant with a machine gun and a clerk, we start our walk.

"What unit are you?"

"Panzergrenadier Division 37"

"Infantry Regiment 535."

There are so many tired, disillusioned, exhausted men. Thousands of them. The beaten defenders of the Alpine Fortress. Sitting on and below a low stone fence are some of my friends. Jelinek, Kaplanek, and Goettler sit gaping at the strange apparition of Americans and me passing by. I want to run to them, but that would wreck my cover and my chances of getting out of here.

We return to the command post for a rest. I am given some cookies and a drink in a tin can. Coca-Cola it is called. Awful tasting stuff, but I dutifully gulp it down. After about half an hour, the colonel calls for me again.

"Mind helping us some more?"

This time I ride with a lieutenant in one of the square cars, a vehicle not unlike our Kübelwagen, but stronger and larger.

"What is your unit?"

A few hundred SS sit miserably in a very wet meadow, feeling punished for what they are. Ambulances pick up the wounded. More ambulances come from the south, over the pass. Quite a few prisoners are bandaged. I wonder what they think when I question them.

"What is your unit?"

A mini Quisling (Collaborator)?

But the war is over, and the Führer is dead. Here we have the Americans, not the Russians nor the French. When I get back to the command post, the Americans have found a German-speaking soldier in their unit.

"Thank you for helping us. We are not prepared to support so many prisoners. We will soon be releasing the army's soldiers who have family members in our occupation zone. Now, you wanted to go somewhere?"

"To my mother."

"Where is you mother, boy?"

"In Aigen-Schlägl, north of Linz, Mister Commander."

He looks at the map on the wall, studded with coloured pins and notes.

"We have a unit going there in the morning. We can give you a ride."

I spend the night sitting on a chair being fed new foods, some of them rather tasty, and practicing my fractured English. In the morning, I am given a box called a K-Ration for sustenance on the ride.

I climb up into the back of a truck with benches on each side. Ten soldiers are riding with me. Off we go, for my very last chapter in this awful war. The truck has a tarpaulin cover, but the back is open, so I can see where we are and know what is going on.

"What is your name, boy?"

Speaking very slowly and enunciating strongly, I answer. "My name is Fredi."

"I am Jack and this is Tom Robert." They all say their names one after the other. "You like chocolate?"

I have not even dreamt about chocolate in ages.

"Yes, please!" The chocolate melts in my mouth. Heaven. "No chocolate since 1938."

"No chocolate for how long?!?"

They all rummage in their knapsacks, and I end up with five bars of real, delicious chocolate.

"Where are you from?"

"Vienna."

"Blue Danube Waltz?"

"Where are you from?"

He lists their hometowns, pointing. "Chicago, Chicago, Texas, New York, Boston, Tennessee, Louisiana, Ohio, Cleveland, San Francisco."

"Chicago, Al Capone?"

"Not anymore."

The traffic is almost all military—very few civilian vehicles. The soldiers are very friendly and tease me about my English. If they are all like this, I think I am going to like the Americans. We pass the bridge in Linz. The scenery becomes more and more familiar. The truck stops right in front of my grandparents' house. I get out. To my surprise, the house has become the American headquarters.

"You be a good boy, Fredi."

"Nice to have met you, Fredi."

"Maybe someday you can come to New York."

"Fredi, you are back!" Frau Gillesberger says. "Your mother is living with the Märzingers now."

I run down the block. Right in front of the Märzinger house, my mother is walking with a pram.

"Fredi, you are alive!"

We embrace and I hug my baby sister. Hallelujah! The war is now really over. The nightmare has ended.

I am again with my family

AUTHOR'S NOTE

Man is the measure of all things. When a man must die, a quick and dignified death avoids agony. Does the same not hold true for the life of a country? If a war becomes irrevocably lost, should there not be an obligation to avoid unnecessary death? In the last stage of the war, Hitler created what became a monstrosity, the Hitler Youth Companies. Led by seventeen and eighteen year olds, military ambition became their driving force. Iron Crosses were more important than lives.

In Vienna, the chaotic changing of commanding generals gave the Hitler Youth Companies free rein to operate behind enemy lines, successfully destroying scores of tanks but at the cost of hundreds of young boys' lives. Much of the destruction in Vienna, as well as in the historic part of Bratislava, was caused by these commandos. I only found out about this after finishing this book.

I was very, very lucky. My immediate leadership, mere boys themselves, was more concerned about our welfare. We grew up together, and they did everything possible to keep us away from the front, let alone become commandos. I am very grateful to them for saving my life under their leadership. We did not lose a single boy in our immediate group.

In another book that I read, one of the commando leaders proudly describes a scene where a fourteen year old under fire screams, "I want to go home! I want to go to my mother!" and the leader coldly shot him. Reading that makes me feel very, very sad but also very lucky. It could have been me.

I honour the following three men who gave their lives
for love of their city:
Major Karl Biedermann
Hauptmann Alfred Huth
Oberleutnant Rudolf Raschke

Hundreds of grieving Austrian mothers
did not see their young sons grow into men.

About the Author

Born in Vienna, in 1929, to a comfortable middle-class family, I did not suffer through the depression. My involvement in the Second World War forms the entirety of this book. I attended the Academy of Applied Art in Vienna. I emigrated to Canada in 1956 and, after about twenty different jobs, I went back to school. I attended a technical college in Vancouver, British Columbia, and graduated from the Vancouver School of Art.

From 1968 until my eighty second birthday, I operated a successful design, graphic art, and marketing business. Widowed, I have one son, two daughters, six grandchildren, and one great-grand-child on the way. I have travelled extensively and am multi-lingual.

A confession to my fellow super-seniors. I am ninety two as of this writing. After a year of Covid-19 lockdown, I had reached the point where it became hard to write a cheque and I had senior moments galore. My then ninety five year old cousin, a writer and musician, told me to start writing. So I did. First in letters to him, up to thirty pages at a time, to the point where I started to write this book. It has not helped me with numbers and appointments, but I can again hold conversations with ease.

My advice to you is this:
Write, it is great therapy.

SPECIAL THANKS

Special thanks to my editor, Jamie Hillegonds, for her friendship and her excellent work, suggestions, and understanding of this difficult material.

Many thanks go out to my computer advisor and typist, Sandra Bowen, who became exceptional at deciphering my hieroglyphics.

A special thanks to Barb Drozdowich of Bakerview Consulting who made my entry into Amazon's publishing world possible.

Manufactured by Amazon.ca
Bolton, ON

30996942R00081